Open Road's

LONDON
with Kids

by Valerie Gwinner

Open Road Family Travel Guides
The only travel guide your family needs!

"I used this book to help plan a recent family trip to London. It was very useful and gave some great ideas about things to do with kids of various ages. I've been to London a few times before, but never with children, so I wanted a book that would give us ideas on kid friendly activities. This was great in that regard...." — *amazon.com*

Open Road Publishing

Open Road's new travel guides cut to the chase.
You don't need a huge travel encyclopedia – you need a
selective guide to steer you right. If you're going on vacation for
a few weeks or less, get a guide that brings you the *best* of any
destination for the amount of time you *really* have for your trip!

Open Road – the guide you need for the family trip you want.

The New Open Road **Family** Travel Guides
Right to the point
Uncluttered
Easy

2nd Revised Edition

OPEN ROAD PUBLISHING
P.O. Box 284, Cold Spring Harbor, NY 11724
www.openroadguides.com

Text Copyright©2011 by Valerie Gwinner
Maps by Andy Herbach
- All Rights Reserved -

ISBN 13: 978-1-59360-131-7
ISBN 10: 1-59360-131-X
Library of Congress Control No. 2010909600

About the Author
Valerie Gwinner is also the author of *Open Road's Paris with Kids.*

For photo credits turn to page 171.

CONTENTS
– Chapter Highlights in Italics –

Maps

1. INTRODUCTION

Charles Dickens referred to **London** as his "magic lantern" — one filled with scenes from his long walks across the city that illuminated his literary thoughts and writings. For the contemporary traveler, there is still something magical about London; it is the magic of Mary Poppins, Tinkerbell, C.S. Lewis, and Platform 9 3/4. London is a place full of familiar images, like those projected in a magic lantern, that have marked our youths and continue to make up an important part of our cultural references. It is the home of Winnie the Pooh, Big Ben, Shakespeare, and Eliza Doolittle. It's the city of double-decker buses, the six wives of Henry VIII, and the 101 Dalmations. All these and many others of the sights and activities that London has to offer help ensure that the magic of London remains — and that whether you are a first time or frequent visitor, the city does not disappoint.

For American visitors, London is also a wonderful destination because it is both exotic and familiar. The architecture, traditions, and foods are different without feeling terribly foreign. You can read all the signs, figure out the menus, and converse with the locals, but still laugh over differences in words and accents. For children, London is a fun place to visit, because there are so many kid-friendly things to see and do. Whether your child prefers to romp in Princess Diana's playground, take a *flight* on the London Eye, get scared by gory scenes at the London Dungeon, or shop till they drop you'll find plenty to do here to keep them entertained.

London is also a vibrant and cosmopolitan place that attracts people from all over the world. To walk the London streets is to experience a great mix of cultures and ethnicities – a Caribbean festival in Notting Hill, Chinese food in Chelsea, or a Bengali deli on Brick

Lane. It is a city rich in theater and music — with shows to please every taste from age 2 to 92. London has beautiful parks where families can frolic undisturbed. There are magnificent museums rich with kid-friendly resources to spark the imagination of even the most flat-footed tourists. There are splendid department stores and funky street markets. There are street performers and mysterious ghosts. There are palaces and boat rides and scary stories, too. There are traces of Paddington Bear, Peter Pan, and Harry Potter's Knight Bus.

All these and more are described within the pages of this book. You'll also find tips for making a visit to a palace or museum into a fun-filled family adventure. There are recommendations for kid-friendly hotels and restaurants, and places to find a light meal or snack. Also included are facts, legends, and anecdotes that bring the stories of London to life for kids and adults. It's as if we could still look through Dickens' lantern and share the magic that is London – With Kids.

2. OVERVIEW

Make it a Great Adventure

Don't be intimidated by the idea of bringing your kids on a trip. With a little preparation, you'll find that traveling with kids can actually make for a great adventure. First of all, discovering a new place and culture with your children can be highly rewarding and supply family memories that last a lifetime. It's a chance to connect with each other without the distractions of home, to try out new things, and to just enjoy being together. You may even discover, as we have, that your kids can become your favorite travel companions. If that's not reason enough to pack up the family bags, here are a few more:

Children bring new perspectives to your travels. They see the world from a different angle. Kids point out details we might miss, such as how the Coca Cola tastes different, the sidewalks are wider, or that there are more mopeds and motorcycles than at home.

Kids take you places you might otherwise skip, but secretly enjoy: the Peter Pan-inspired playground in Kensington Park, the gory depths of the London Dungeon, or a canal boat ride to the London Zoo. London museums offer terrific kids' activities and tours that can make a museum visit more fun and enlightening for everyone. Kids also give you permission to try things you might be embarrassed to do at home, like perform a cartwheel in the middle of Hyde Park.

Traveling with kids helps break down cultural barriers. It gives you something in common with other parents, and it brings out the kid-lovers in people who don't have children of their own.

Finally, traveling with children reminds us that it's okay to slow down. Enjoy the city at a human pace. Take an afternoon nap. Have a leisurely cup of tea while the kids quietly play in the hotel room. Spend some time watching the world go by from a park bench or café terrace. After all, you're on vacation.

Involve Your Kids

Children will be much more enthusiastic about traveling to London if you give them in role in the planning process – remember it's their trip, too. Even small kids can feel like they are part of the action if you include them in some background research. One of the best methods with young children is to introduce them to the city ahead of time with books and videos that feature London. (See below for a list of suggestions.) It gives them a taste of what is ahead and things to look forward to.

With small children, you can bring along books such as AA Milne's *When We Were Very Young*, *A Bear Named Paddington*, or *Madeleine in London* and see how many sights you can recognize from the illustrations. You can also read chapter books together such as *Peter Pan*, *Harry Potter*, or *The Lion, the Witch and the Wardrobe* that have references to places in London and help put everyone in an English mood. You'll find references to many of the characters and adventures of those books within the pages of this guidebook.

If your children are older, encourage them to help plan your itinerary. You don't have to build your entire trip around their ideas, but you can give them a chance to pick their top choices. Cater to their interests.

For example:

- **Is your daughter a fashion slave?** Go for a canal boat ride up Regents Canal to Camden Town with its endless markets of vintage and funky clothes. For more high-brow tastes, visit the gown exhibit in Kensington Palace then head to Harrods – the nec plus ultra in fancy shopping.

- **Is your child a budding scientist?** Try some of the great kids' activities at the Museum of Natural History or Science Museum and end the day chasing the giant pigeons in Kensington Gardens.

- **Any future sailors in your group?** Take a boat trip down the Thames to Greenwich's Maritime Museum where you can test your nautical skills. While there climb aboard the *Cutty Sark* clipper ship and go up to the Royal Observatory where you can stand right on the Greenwich Meridian Line.

- **Are your kids crazy about the Harry Potter stories?** Take a ride on top of a double-decker bus (you'll feel like you're on the Knight Bus) and visit Platform 9 3/4 in the Kings Cross Train Station. You can even take a train to Windsor and visit a real English boarding school at Eton (the one both Princes William and Harry attended).

- **Does your son or daughter have a dramatic flair?** Take them for a tour of Shakespeare's Globe Theatre, teach them a few Shakespearean insults (you'll find some in this book), and treat yourselves to a London show – there's one for every taste.

Balance Everyone's Desires

The secret to a successful family trip is to find ways to have something for everyone. If you build your whole trip around your children's desires, you will come home exhausted and frustrated. Similarly you can't expect a child to love London if he or she is forced to sit through endlessly long meals, wait for you to try on clothes in one store after another, or visit countless museums at a crawling pace. London is dotted with great parks, pastry shops, and fun boutiques that spark kids' imaginations. It's easy to intersperse these with visits to museums, monuments, or other sights. Kids also love riding on a double-decker bus, taking a boat tour, or enjoying views from high places, so build these into your sightseeing plans, too.

However, don't forget to incorporate your own tastes and interests. Children like to mimic and model adults, and it is surprising how often they will rise to the occasion when taken on a grownup outing. For example, our kids loved going to the theater with us, laughing hard when we saw the Reduced Shakespeare Company and standing for hours as groundlings at Shakespeare's Globe.

Make Museums & Palaces Fun

Few kids or adults can stand going through every room of a museum or palace at a snail's rate. Fortunately, there are lots of ways to make both of these places entertaining. This is especially true in London where they go to great lengths to be family-friendly. It is even true for museums such as the Victoria and Albert Museum or National Portrait Gallery that may sound like a snooze, but end up being highlights of the trip. You will see detailed listings of kid-oriented activities in each of the London museums and palaces described in this book.

Here are a few general suggestions for making museums and palaces fun:

- **Take advantage of the kid-friendly activities that they offer.** Many museums/palaces offer treasure hunts, activity guides, and family-friendly tours. There are also dress-up clothes, activity filled backpacks, interactive exhibits, funny demonstrations, and arts/crafts. Be sure to ask about kids activities and special events at the information desk. You'll be surprised how much grown-ups can learn from them, too.

- **Make your own treasure hunt.** Check out the museum's web site ahead of time or visit the post cards at the gift shop and pick out some favorite items your kids want to hunt down. Several museums have computer rooms where you can design your own scavenger hunt, based on their collections. You can also cater a hunt to your kids' tastes: for example looking for depictions of monsters, children, animals, sports, machines, etc.
- **Give your kids a lesson in navigation by handing them a** copy of the museum's map (distributed for free at the entrance) **and following their lead.** Some, such as the British Museum, offer special children's maps.
- **Rent audioguides for your children.** Many sites offer special ones for kids. They appeal to their natural love of gadgets, help children feel empowered, and let them enjoy a private tour at their own pace.
- **Cater to kids' interests.** London's museums and palaces offer a range of things to see such as weapons and armor, buses and trains, ships, dolls/dollhouses, fashion, musical instruments, scientific exhibits, animals, mazes, ghosts, and more.
- **Play "pick your favorite"** – encourage your kids to choose which paintings, pieces of furniture, or objects they would put in their room if they could. Which armor would they wear if they were knights? Which king or queen would they want to be? Which room would they want to sleep in if this was their palace?
- **Go for gore.** Really! Kids are fascinated by tales of monsters, Black plague, torture, and the like. You will find plenty of examples of these in the Tower of London, London Dungeon, Madame Tussaud's, and other museums and palaces in the city.
- **Surf online before you go.** The major museums and palaces have websites that your kids can browse through to pick out what they'd like to see.
- **Take a break during your visit.** Most museums and palaces have cafés where you can refuel and rest weary feet.

• **Divide and conquer**. If part of your group just can't bear the idea of another museum or palace, split up. Let one adult have a few hours of culture while the rest of the group goes on a boat tour, plays in a park, or does some shopping.

Getting Oriented

London is big! It's about twice the size of Paris or New York City — with a population of 7.2 million people. London is also a collection of neighborhoods, originally distinct villages, which still retain some of their original character and charm.

Even though London is very spread out, it is relatively easy to find your way around. The city is divided into postal code districts, which reflect where they sit, compared to the center of the city. The letters of the codes stand for compass directions, east-west-north-south; the letter "C" indicates you are near the center; and the numbers tell you how close the area is to the center of the city (with lower numbers being closest in). Thus for example, WC1 stands for west-central near the center. These postal codes are conveniently indicated on street addresses and on most street signs to help you find your way around. In addition, it's important to note that the vast majority of the sights you will want to visit in London tend to be clustered in the central parts of the city. This means that in spite of the city's vast size, you will spend most of your time within a smaller, central perimeter.

Here's a description of what you'll find in London's more central neighborhoods, according to their postal codes:

W1: West End - Theaters, Mayfair, Marylebone, Piccadilly Circus, Marble Arch, Soho, Wellington Arch, Regent Street, Oxford Street, St. James Church, Chinatown, Baker Street, plush shopping district.

W2: Paddington and Bayswater - Hyde Park, Paddington Train Station, Heathrow Express Train, Bayswater Road.

W8: Kensington - Kensington Gardens and Palace, Princess Diana Memorial Playground, fancy stores.

WC1: Bloomsbury - British Museum, British Library, Charles Dickens' House, Corams' Fields Playground, Sir John Soane's Museum, University of London, St. Pancras Train Station, King's Cross Train Station, Euston Train Station.

WC2: Covent Garden and Trafalgar Square, St. Martin's in the Field Church, National Gallery, National Portrait Gallery, Leicester Square.

SW1: Belgravia, Knightsbridge, Pimlico, Victoria - Buckingham Palace, Westminster Abbey, Houses of Parliament, Whitehall, Big Ben,

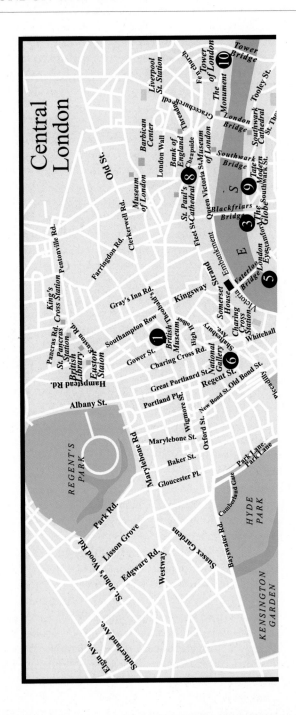

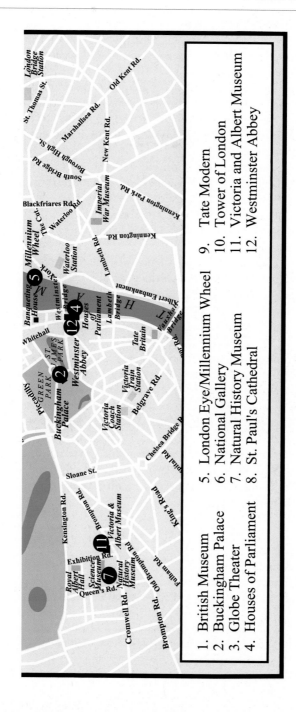

1. British Museum
2. Buckingham Palace
3. Globe Theater
4. Houses of Parliament
5. London Eye/Millennium Wheel
6. National Gallery
7. Natural History Museum
8. St. Paul's Cathedral
9. Tate Modern
10. Tower of London
11. Victoria and Albert Museum
12. Westminster Abbey

Cabinet War Rooms, 10 Downing Street, Royal Mews, Green Park, St. James' Park, Tate Britain, Harrods, Sloane Street and Beauchamp Place shops, Victoria Train Station.

SW3: Chelsea - Cheyne Walk of literary London, flower and garden show, Physic Garden (botanical garden), King's Road boutiques, Chelsea pensioners, Sloane Street.

SW5: Earl's Court - Many bed and breakfasts, hotels, direct tube line to Heathrow Airport.

SW7: South Kensington - Kensington Gardens, Hyde Park, Natural History Museum, Science Museum, Victoria and Albert Museum, Albert Memorial, Royal Albert Hall, Baden-Powell House.

NW1: Regent's Park - Regent's Park, London Planetarium, Madame Tussauds' London Zoo, British Library, Sherlock Holmes Museum, Regent's Canal.

EC1-EC2: Farringdon and Clerkenwell - Barbican Center, Roman Wall, Museum of London, Smithfield Market.

EC4: The City - St. Paul's Cathedral, The Monument, Fleet Street and financial district.

E1: East End – Brick Lane Market, Bethnal Green Museum of Childhood, Spitalfields Market, Petticoat Lane Street Market

SE1: South Bank and Waterloo - Tower Bridge, Shakespeare's Globe Theater, Golden Hinde, London Eye, Southwark Cathedral, Imperial War Museum, Waterloo Bridge, Tate Modern, Millennium Bridge, Waterloo Station, London Bridge, London Dungeon, Borough Market, Hayes Galleria, Florence Nightingale Museum, Dali Universe, London Aquarium.

SE10: Greenwich – Cutty Sark, Maritime Museum, Royal Observatory, Greenwich Mean Line, Greenwich Park, old village and markets.

NW3: Hampstead – Hampstead Heath park, Hampstead Village, John Keats' house.

SW19: Wimbledon – Tennis Museum and British Open Championship.

Getting Around London

Public transport **Travel Information Centres**, where you can purchase tickets and passes or get maps and information, are located at: Euston Train Station, King's Cross Train Station, Liverpool Train Street and Victoria Train Station, Oxford Circus Tube Station, Piccadilly Tube Station, St. James Park Tube Station, Hammersmith Tube Station, and Heathrow Airport (terminals 1, 2, and 3).

The London Tube: London has an extensive and very reliable subway system known as the Tube or the Underground. Note: Free maps are available in any Tube station. Each Tube line has a name and is color coded: for example the Piccadilly Line that you can take from Heathrow Airport into the city is blue on maps and signs.

Two notes of caution:

• Don't be misled by signs indicating "subway" – these will direct you to an underpass, such as a pedestrian tunnel under a busy street, but not necessarily to the Tube.

• If you are traveling with a stroller or luggage, be aware that not all Tube stations have elevators (called lifts). Most have long escalators.

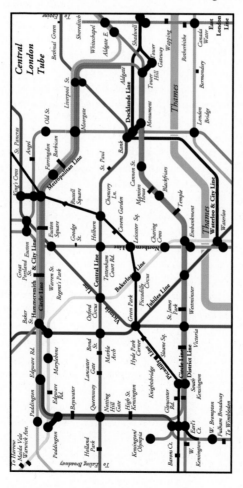

You can buy individual tickets in any Tube station, but you will save a lot of money if you buy a **Family Travelcard, 1-Day Travelcard, Several-Day** or **Weeklong Travelcard**. There are special rates for kids. These allow unlimited access to bus and Tube service all day (although you have to travel after 9:30 am for the Family Pass). On weekends, the Family Travelcard is even cheaper; because kids travel free (they still need a ticket, however, to go through the entrance and exit turnstiles). Children under age 5 travel free on buses and subways any time as long as they are with a paying adult. Older children pay reduced rates during the week.

We found that the Tube station ticket agents were very helpful at recommending the best tickets to buy depending on our travel plans, so don't hesitate to ask. Also, you can sometimes buy a combined Tube + Tourist Site ticket. This may save you both time and money, for example to visit the Tower of London, so it's worth asking.

Make sure to hang on to your tickets. You will need them both to enter and exit the stations. You can also purchase entrance tickets for the Tower of London in the Tube stations, saving you from a long line at the entrance.

Double-Decker and Other Public Buses: This is one of the best, and most economical, experiences in London. The top level, especially if you can sit in the front seat, is just plain fun. You get a great view of the city and can marvel from up high at how the drivers manage to navigate crowded traffic and tight streets. The occasional sudden stops and narrow turns made us feel like we were riding on Harry Potter's Night Bus. The one down side to riding the bus is that it can be slow, especially during rush hour, due to traffic congestion. So if you are in a hurry, take the Tube. Otherwise, take the bus enjoy the ride and the sites.

Children under age 11 ride for free on buses. You can purchase tickets in any Tube station, but you will save money by purchasing a Family Travelcard (good for travel all-day on buses and subways) or 1-Day bus pass. These can be purchased in any Tube station or travel information center. Free bus maps are available in Tube stations and travel information centers.

Docklands Light Railway (DLR). This is a more recent addition to London's excellent public transportation system. It consists of automated trains that head east along the Thames from the center of the city. You can use the DLR to visit the Isle of Dogs or Greenwich.

Double-Decker Tour Buses: Three companies offer 1-day passes on tour buses that allow you to hop on and off at will during the day. They include the Big Bus Company, London Pride, and the Original London Sightseeing Tour. You can purchase tickets wherever the bus stops, including Trafalgar Square. Although it's always fun to ride on the top deck and listen to a commentary of the city, we found that this was an expensive way to see the sights. You can enjoy many of the same views from a public double-decker bus, for a fraction of the cost of a private tour bus. That said, a double-decker tour bus may be a good alternative if you have only one day to see London or if you are traveling with someone who has trouble getting around.

Taxis: A ride in a London Cab is really a pleasure. The taxis are big and roomy (you can fit a whole stroller inside) and the cab drivers are friendly and helpful. The drivers have to pass a complicated exam testing their knowledge of the city in order to obtain a taxi license, so you can be sure they'll know their way around. Unfortunately, London Cabs are also very expensive, so it's best to think of them as a luxury and use them sparingly. Note: If you leave something behind in a taxi, you can call the lost property office at 200 Baker Street (Baker Street Tube) at 020 7918 2000.

Walking: Even though London is huge, many of the sights you will want to visit are clustered in central parts of the city, within walking distance of each other. So bring good walking shoes and enjoy the exercise. If you are traveling with babies or toddlers, consider bringing a sturdy, lightweight stroller that you can fold up easily.

Driving: The first time we visited London with kids, we arrived by car through the Chunnel from France. The harrowing experience of driving on the left without getting killed was enough to convince us to leave the car in our friends' Hampstead driveway and rely instead on the excellent public transportation and taxi systems of London. There are other good reasons to avoid driving in London, too: central London is now subject to a special congestion tax, fuel is very expensive, and parking is next to impossible. So, leave the car behind or use it only for excursions out of the city.

Boat Rides: This is a great way to view some of the major sights of London or to visit places like Greenwich and Hampton Court Palace. Numerous companies offer trips up and down the Thames River or along some of London's lovely canals:

- **London River Services** (part of the Public Transportation Service). *Tel. 020 7222 1234; www.tfl.gov.uk* . Service goes from Hampton Court, Richmond, and Kew in the west, through 17 London stops, to Greenwich and the Thames Barrier in the east. City stops include Tower Pier, London Bridge, Bankside Pier, Blackfriars Millennium Pier, Savoy Pier, Festival Pier, Embankment Pier, Waterloo Pier, Westminster Pier, and Chelsea Harbor Pier. Fares vary depending on the distance, but kids 5-15 are half-price, and kids under 5 are free.

- **Westminster-Greenwich Thames Passenger Boat Service**, *Westminster Pier, Victoria Embankment, SW1. Tel. 020 7839 3572.* Tours go down river from Westminster Pier to Greenwich (50 minute ride). Departures every 30-40 minutes, 10-4 (winter), 10:30-5 (summer).
- **Westminster Passenger Association.** *Westminster Pier, Victoria Embankment, SW1. Tel. 020 7930 2062, Web: www.wpsa.co.uk/index.html.* Tours head upstream from Westminster Bridge to Kew, Richmond, and Hampton Court, April through October. Count on 1.5 hours for Kew, 2 1/2 to 4 hours for Hampton Court depending on tides. Departure times may vary depending on the tides, so it's best to check via phone or internet.
- **River Cruises.** *Tel. 020 7987 1185.* Boats leave from Embankment, Waterloo, Bankside, Tower of London, and Greenwich. You can opt for point-to-point rides (fare vary according to distance and whether 1-way or round trip) or a 50-minute circular cruise from Westminster Pier (Adults £8.70; Kids £4.40; Family £28).
- **London Ducktours**, County Hall (By the London Eye). *Tube: Waterloo. Tel. 020 7928 3132. Online: www.londonducktours.co.uk .* Open daily. Tours last 70 minutes. You'll ride on amphibious DUK boats designed for the D-Day landings in WWII. It's a fun way to see both land and riverside sights in London. Adults £20; Kids £14-16, depending on age; Families (2 adults + 2 kids) £58.
- **Regent's Canal Boat Trips.** *London Waterbus Company. Camden Lock Place, NW1.* Four historic canal boats offer guided tours along London's canals between Camden Lock, Little Venice, and the London Zoo. Hourly departures from 10-5 (Apr-Sept), 3 departures per day (Oct-Mar). Adult £9; Kids 3-15 years £4.50; Infants under 3 years are free; Family (2 adults + 2 children) £22.50; Students £7. You can also buy a ticket that includes entrance to the zoo.
- **Jason's Canal Boat Trip.** *Jason's Wharf, Blomfield Road, (opposite #60), Little Venice, London W9. Tel. 020 7286 3428.* One-way and round-trips are offered along Regent's Canal to Camden Town. Departures at 10:30, 12:30, 2:30 (4:30 Sat-Sun) Apr-Sep. Adults £8.50; Kids £4.50

3. THE CITY

SAINT PAUL'S, MUSEUM OF LONDON, & BARBICAN

During Roman Times, the city of Londinium measured about one square mile and was surrounded by a protective defense wall. Today, that section of London is still called "The City" and represents not only its historical core but also the country's financial center. It is here that you will find the Bank of England, Lloyd's of London, and the London Stock Exchange. Fortunately for visiting families, that's not all this part of the city has to offer. There's also the kid-friendly Museum of London, St. Paul's Cathedral, The Monument to the Great London Fire, and the Barbican Centre for the Arts.

Museum of London, 1 London Wall, London EC2. (The museum entrance is one story above the street level. There is access by stairs, escalator, or lift from the London Wall/St Martin's le Grand/Aldersgate Street roundabout.) Tube: Barbican or St. Paul's. Open Mon-Sat 10-6, Sun 12-6. Admission is free.

Note: This museum has an excellent series of **World City Activity Sheets** for kids. There are also kid-friendly activities, performances, and workshops on weekends and during school vacations.

The Museum of London traces the city's history from prehistoric times to the 20th century. Appropriately enough it is built in the area where early London first began; you can see traces of the old Roman City Wall from the museum's galleries. It's a great museum to visit with kids! There are fun, interactive exhibits, especially in the upstairs galleries devoted to Prehistoric and Roman London. There are also interesting reconstructions of houses and shops from different periods. You'll see how prehistoric settlers lived, learn that Caesar's army camped where Heathrow Airport is now located, and admire jewels buried during the Tudor period only to be recovered centuries later. A sound and lights exhibit describes the Great London Fire of 1666.

The dazzling Lord Mayor's Coach is on display downstairs. Built in 1757 it is taken out once a year for the Lord Mayor's Show – a ceremony dating from 1215 in which the Mayor of London swears allegiance to the Queen.

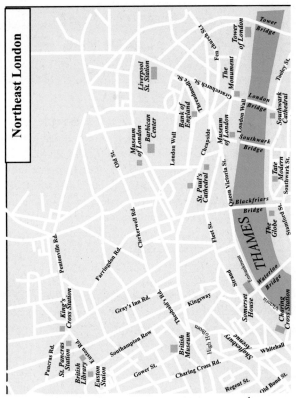

Galleries on the lower floor feature recreations of 18th century Prison gates and cells, as well as examples of clothing styles, common diseases, and children's toys.

Interactive computers offer more information, and friendly museum staff put on fun performances to bring history further to life. The museum has an excellent gift shop and good café with kids' meals and junior portions.

St. Paul's Cathedral. *Saint Paul's Churchyard, EC4. Tube: St. Paul's. Open to visitors Mon-Sat, 8:30-4. Adults: £11; Kids under 16: £3.50; Families (2 adults and 2 children): £25.50; Students: £8.50. Additional charge if you want a guided tour. Audio-tours of the Cathedral and Crypt are available for £4.*

Note: Saint Paul's is an Anglican Church. Daily services are held at 7:30 (Mattins and Litany); 8 (Holy Communion); 12:30 (Holy Communion), and 5 (Evensong). On Sunday there are services at 8, 10:15, 11:30, 3:15, and 6, along with occasional organ recitals at 5.

Saint Paul's Cathedral is where great events are celebrated, such as royal weddings or state funerals. It has been the site of the city's main cathedral for hundreds of years. The first Saint Paul's was built in 604 AD, burned to the ground in 675, was rebuilt, and then thoroughly ransacked by invading Vikings in 962. Work began on a new cathedral in 1087, taking 200 years to complete. In 1666, it was completely destroyed in the Great London Fire. The building you see today was designed by the famous architect, Christopher Wren. Its construction began in 1675.

Wren is said to have inspected the work daily. To check out the building of the cathedral's Dome, he was pulled up and down the construction site in a basket. The last stone was placed into position by his son in 1708 – on the day of Wren's 76th birthday.

The interior of the church is surprisingly bare, considering its importance. The mosaics were installed during the reign of Queen Victoria, who declared that Saint Paul's was too dreary. To the left as you enter is the **Chapel of All Souls**. It was dedicated in 1925 to the memory of Field Marshal Lord Kitchener (1850-1916) and to all the soldiers who lost their lives during World War I. There are sculptures of Saint Michael (patron saint of soldiers) and Saint George (patron saint of England) – both of whom were legendary dragon slayers. There is a statue of Lord Kitchener and silver-plated candlesticks on the altar that were made from melted-down trophies won by the London Rifle Brigade.

In the Nave (the long central part of the cathedral), on the northern side there is a large **monument to the Duke of Wellington**, who defeated Napoleon's forces in the Battle of Waterloo. He is depicted on horseback at the top of the monument, and his coffin is held within a large granite tomb. Wellington was known as The Iron Duke, for being such a tireless leader in battle. He is commemorated in everyday items such as Beef Wellington, Wellington Cigars, and rubber rain boots that the British call "Wellies."

Under the Dome to your right in the South Transept is a **monument to Admiral Nelson**, the great British naval hero who died in the Battle of Trafalgar in 1805. Nelson is depicted leaning on an anchor. The lion sculpture at the base of the monument symbolizes the fact that he died in battle. Nelson's coffin was made from the mast of a French ship that he sank in an earlier battle. It is nestled inside a lead coffin, which is in turn held within a stone sarcophagus. There are also memorials to the famous English painter, **JMW Turner** and to **Captain Robert Scott**, the great explorer who died on a South Pole expedition in 1912.

The organ dates from 1695. It contains 7,189 pipes, five keyboards, and 138 organ stops.

The apse (the rounded section behind the Alter) holds the **American Memorial Chapel**, dedicated to the American servicemen and women stationed in Britain who died in World War II. There are more than 28,000 names on the roll of honor. The windows feature themes of sacrifice and are decorated with insignia representing the 50 United States and the US Armed Forces. In the décor of the wooden paneling you can see a rocket, which is a tribute to the US Space Program.

Saint Paul's is famous for its **golden dome**. Outside, at the very top, you can see a golden ball (which is 6 feet across) and golden cross that stands 365 feet above the ground. The ball and cross together measure 23 feet high and weigh nearly 7 tons. The dome contains a series of interior and exterior galleries, which run around its perimeter. The **Golden Gallery** circles the highest point of the outer dome. It is 280 feet above the ground and can be reached by climbing up 530 steps. For those who aren't afraid of heights, it offers a spectacular 360-degree view of London. Inside the dome, you can climb up the 259 steps to the **Whispering Gallery** where you can view the inside of the Cathedral from up high. You can also admire its acoustical effects. Due to the curve of the dome, even if you stand on opposite sides of the whispering gallery, you can still hear each other whisper.

There are two entrances to the **crypt** on either side of the Transept (the t-shaped sections under the dome). Inside the crypt is a memorial dedicated to **Sir Christopher Wren**. Next to his tomb you can see a stone bearing his architect's mark. Members of his family are buried near him. Other tombs in the crypt memorialize famous people, such as Sir Alexander Fleming, the man who discovered penicillin; Sir Arthur Sullivan (of Gilbert and Sullivan fame) and the sculptor Henry Moore.

The Cathedral's **Treasury** was robbed in 1810 and lost most of its ceremonial gold and silver objects. As a result, the vessels and other church treasures displayed here today are nearly all on loan from churches throughout London. There is an exhibit by the treasury dedicated to the Great Fire of 1666 and its devastating damage.

Saint Paul's contains two restaurants. The **Refectory Restaurant**, *open daily 11:30-5*, serves lunch and afternoon tea. On Sunday, there is a traditional British Roast Lunch. The **Crypt Café**, *open daily 9-5 (10-5 on Sun)* serves soups, salads, sandwiches, and home-made pastries.

Barbican Centre. *Silk Street, EC2. Tube: Barbican or Moorgate. Box Office opens 10-8 daily. Tel. 020 7638 8891. You can ask the box office about backstage tours.*

The Barbican neighborhood is a modern complex built on a site that was leveled by German bombs in World War II. It contains apartments, gardens, shops, and restaurants, as well as this big center for the arts. The Barbican Centre regularly hosts two of London's most famous cultural institutions: the **London Symphony Orchestra** (over 90 concerts a year) and the **Royal Shakespeare Company** (performances Oct-May). It is also a major venue for dance, film, and art exhibits. The Centre contains three large performance spaces, several art galleries, two multi-screen cinemas, a greenhouse, a library, and several cafés and restaurants.

Smithfield Market. *Charterhouse Street, EC1. Tube: Barbican or Farringdon. Open Mon-Thur 4am-10am.*

This lively wholesale meat market was once the sight of the annual Saint Bartholomew's Fair. The "smooth field" from which the name is derived was also used for jousting tournaments and public executions. Hundreds of Protestants were burned at the stake here on orders of Queen Mary I (also known as Bloody Mary). William Wallace the Scottish hero (portrayed by Mel Gibson in the movie *Braveheart*) was drawn and quartered here – a particularly gruesome form of execution in which the prisoner was disemboweled then cut to pieces. Another terrible form of execution was experienced here by the Bishop of Greenwich. He was locked in a cage held over a fire at Smithfield for refusing to recognize Henry VIII as the head of the Church of England, after Henry broke off from the Catholic Church in order to divorce his first wife.

Today, the market buzzes with butchers and buyers in the early hours of the day. The market buildings were recently restored to their original vivid colors.

Saint Bartholomew's Hospital. *Next to Smithfield Market. EC1.*

This is said to be the oldest hospital in Britain. By some accounts it received wounded Saxon soldiers from the Battle of Hastings against William the Conqueror in 1066. By other accounts it is slightly more recent, founded in the 12th century, and received wounded soldiers from famous battles such as Crécy, Agincourt, Waterloo, and the Crimean War.

Across from St. Bartholomew's Hospital, on the corner of Giltspur Street and Cock Lane, there is a statue set high in the building called the **Golden Boy**. It marks the spot where the Great Fire of London (1666) is said to have stopped.

St. Bartholomew-The-Great Church. *West Smithfield. By Smithfield Market. EC1. Tube: Barbican.*

This church was founded in 1123, though much has been rebuilt over time. In 1725, Benjamin Franklin used the church's chapel as a workshop and printing room. The Butchers Company from nearby Smithfield Market holds an annual service here.

Guildhall. *Gresham Street. EC2. Tube: Bank.*

This impressive building has been the center of London's City government for 1,000 years. The Lord Mayor's monthly meetings with the Corporation of London's governing body are held here, as are ceremonial events and banquets. In the Guildhall Library there is a small **Clock Museum**. It's just one room but contains over 600 timepieces from the 16th to 19th centuries, including a skull-shaped watch that belonged to Mary, Queen of Scots.

St. Mary le Bow. *Bow Lane. EC2. Tube: Bank or St. Pauls. Free lunchtime concerts on Thurs. at 1pm.*

This church, begun according to plans designed by Christopher Wren, is famous for its bells. It is said that a true London Cockney is anyone born within earshot of their ringing. The crypt dates from Norman times and is one of the oldest in London. It contains a vegetarian restaurant called The Place Below that serves fresh breakfasts and lunches.

The Monument (to the Great Fire of London). *Monument Street. Tube: Monument. Open Mon-Fri 10-6; Sat-Sun 2-6. Adults £3; Kids £1. You can also purchase a combined ticket for this monument and the Tower Bridge Exhibition: Adults £8, Kids £3.*

This tower was designed by Sir Christopher Wren to commemorate the Great London Fire of 1666, which burned for three days and destroyed over 13,000 houses. It stands 202 feet high, which is equal to the distance between the Monument and the bakery on Pudding Lane where the fire is said to have begun. The Monument took six years to complete. It is made of stone with a copper urn on top decorated with flames. There is a great view of central London from the top of the tower, if you don't mind the dizzying climb up 311 spiral steps. At the end of your visit, you are entitled to a special certificate with a nice reproduction of the building.

Leadenhall Market. *Gracechurch Street. EC3. Tube: Monument. Open Mon-Fri, 7-4.*

This pretty shopping gallery (*see photo below*) dates from the 1880s, although there has been a market on this spot since Roman times. It has stalls selling fresh fruits, vegetables, meats, and flowers. There are also cafés and restaurants. What impressed us was that most of the shoppers were men in 3-piece suits, a testimony to the fact that this is the heart of London's financial district. We also liked the story of Old Tom, a male goose that escaped the poultry vendor's chopping block in the late 1700s and became a favorite market mascot. He lived for an astonishing 38 years off scraps from local inns. When Old Tom finally died of natural causes, he was buried in the market hall.

St. Magnus the Martyr Church. *Lower Thames Street. EC3. Tube: Monument.*

This church was designed by Sir Christopher Wren. It has a beautiful steeple with an octagonal lantern at the top. Free concerts are performed on Tuesdays at 1pm.

4. TOWER OF LONDON/ TOWER BRIDGE

These are two of London's most famous landmarks. The Tower Bridge provides a beautiful gateway to central London. The Tower fortress stands guard over crown jewels, sacred ravens, and the ghosts of its own bloody past.

Tower of London, *Tower Hill, Tube: Tower Hill. Open daily 9-5 (10-5 on Sundays) from Mar-Oct, and 9-4 (10-4 on Sundays) from Nov-Feb. Entrance: Family (up to 2 adults and 3 kids) £47; Adults £17; Kids under 16 £9.50; students £14.50. Joint tickets for the Tower and Hampton Court or Kensington Palace are also available.*

Note: You can save money booking ahead of time on-line or by buying the London Pass. You can watch a **Changing of the Guard** each day on the Tower Green at 11:30. An audioguide is available for £4.

This is one of London's most famous sites, attracting 2.5 million visitors each year. The Tower of London offers gory history, interesting tour guides, huge black ravens, and glittery Crown Jewels – no wonder it's such a hit. The building itself is impressive with its massive turreted walls and stark towers. It was first built nearly a thousand years ago by **William the Conqueror**, victor of the Battle of Hastings in the year 1066. Formerly the Duke of Normandy in France, William was crowned King of England in Westminster Abbey and began building a castle in London to assert his authority over his new subjects – particularly the feisty Londoners.

William the Conqueror's Tower was a motte and bailey fortress made of timber and daub. It was crafted by Norman masons and Anglo-Saxon builders brought in (forcibly) from the English countryside. The architects were members of the Norman clergy, for they were the ones who knew how to make great stone buildings. The fortress was surrounded by a deep ditch and wooden stockade. William's castle was built along the SE corner of the old Roman City walls at a spot that once held a Roman fort. (Note: You can still see a piece of the Roman Wall by the Tower Hill Tube station.)

The imposing **White Tower** in the middle of the castle was begun during the reign of William the Conqueror and completed by his son, William Rufus. It took 25 years to complete. Standing more than 90 feet high, it dwarfed London's one-story houses and served as both a royal residence and symbol of the king's power. At the base the walls are 15 feet thick, tapering to 11 feet at the top. There was originally only one entrance to the White Tower. It was placed high above the ground and was accessible only from a wooden stairway that could be pulled up if the castle was under attack.

Practical Tips

•Buy your entrance tickets in advance at any tube station, online, or over the phone to avoid the ticket line at the Tower.
•To avoid long lines for the Crown Jewels, go early in the day and make it the first stop on your visit.
•Take advantage of the free, guided tours led by the Yeoman Wardens (Beefeaters). Tours depart every 30 minutes.
• Ask for the free family trail activity guide
• Go to the Tower's website ahead of time to download kid-friendly information, activities, and resources: *www.hrp.org.uk/TowerOfLondonTowerActivitiesforfamilies.aspx*
•There are baby-changing facilities in the restrooms behind the Jewel House. Baby food and kids' menus are available at the New Armouries restaurant.
•Tell your children that if they become lost they should ask for help from a red uniformed Yeoman (Beefeater). Lost children will be taken to the Byward Tower where they can be reunited with their parents.

There are different explanations for the origins of the name White Tower: according to some versions it comes from the fact that the building was white-washed during the reign of King Henry III, who made it his principle residence. Other versions say it was made of white stone, or built on a site formerly called Bryn Gwyn, meaning White Hill in Saxon. The White Tower has only three rooms per story, but they are large. They contain some of England's oldest remaining fireplaces and toilets. You can also see an impressive collection of weapons and armory in this part of the castle, including four increasingly larger suits of armor made to for King Henry VIII, who by the age of 50 had a waistline of 45 inches! There are also suits of armor to fit a child, a dwarf, a giant, a horse, and even an elephant.

Over the years, successive English kings added on to the castle. In the 1190s, Richard the Lionheart's Chancellor enlarged and reinforced the Tower fortress. This did not prevent the invading French forces from setting up quarters in the Tower during the reign of King Henry III (1216-72). He managed to dislodge them, but later had to seek refuge in the Tower himself during baron-led uprisings in 1236 and 1238. Henry III further strengthened the castle's defenses, including the addition of new towers, a moat, and a ring of protective walls all around the White Tower. The Tower's moats were used to slow down invaders, prevent them from digging access tunnels, and to stock fish for food.

Edward I (1272-1307) added a second ring of defensive walls. This was a form of castle architecture brought home from the Crusades and known as a concentric defense. The inner walls were designed to be higher than the outer walls so that archers could shoot arrows from both walls without hitting their comrades. The main entrance to the castle was guarded by three successive gateways and three drawbridges. You can still see the narrow arrow slits (known as loops) and arch openings (known as murder holes from which guards could pour rocks or water on invaders) in the defensive walls and gates.

Edward I's private rooms were in the **Wakefield Tower** (above Traitor's Gate). They represent the only remaining Medieval palace in all of Britain. There are guides in this part of the Tower dressed in period clothes, who will describe medieval life to you and show you the reproductions of period furnishings, including a copy of King Edward's throne.

In 1381, the Tower was stormed by a group of angry, overtaxed farmers led by a man named Wat Tyler. They seized four high-ranking officials, including the Archbishop of Canterbury, Royal Treasurer, a tax official, and a doctor whom they executed on Tower Hill. King Richard II was only 14 years old at the time. He agreed to meet with representatives of the farmers and pretended to meet their demands. In the end, however, Wat Tyler was captured and executed, and the revolt was crushed.

Henry VII (1485-1509) built residential additions to the Lanthorn Tower and designed a garden. When his favorite mistress, Elizabeth of

York, died in childbirth, he had her body laid out in the White Tower, surrounded by 500 candles. His son, Henry VIII (1509-47) added new lodgings for his second wife, Anne Boleyn. Following her execution at the Tower, it was no longer used as a royal residence and became increasingly home to religious and political prisoners.

In 1666 after the Great Fire destroyed much of London, King Charles III opened the walls of the Tower of London to house the city's homeless.

Lion Tower (near the drawbridge) became home to a royal menagerie starting in the 13th century. King Henry II had leopards, an elephant, and a polar bear that caught fish in the castle moat. King James I kept lions in this tower, hence the name. In 1835, the Tower's menagerie was moved to the London Zoo.

The Tower as a Prison. The Tower had first been used as a prison during the reign of Henry III (1216-72). One the first prisoners was a Bishop named Rannulf Flambard. He was imprisoned by King Henri I, but allowed to keep his servants and bags of gold. True to his name, Flambard lived a flamboyant lifestyle in prison, bribing his jailors and throwing parties for them. One night in 1101, he got all the guards drunk during a banquet and escaped by climbing out a window and sliding down a rope to freedom. He was eventually pardoned, returned to being a bishop, and oversaw the completion of the nave of the Durham Cathedral.

In 1483, the 13-year-old heir to the throne Edward V and his younger brother Richard were sent to the Tower as prisoners of their uncle, the Duke of Gloucester. They were never seen again, presumably murdered by their uncle who took over the throne as King Richard III. Years later the remains of two small males were indeed found buried in the Tower grounds.

Another important prisoner of the Tower was Thomas More, who refused to recognize Henry VIII as head of the Church of England, after Henry split from the Catholic Church in order to divorce his first wife. Henry VIII's second wife, Anne Boleyn was imprisoned and executed in the Tower. She had failed to produce a son, giving birth instead to the future Queen Elizabeth I, and was accused of adultery. Catherine Howard, Henry's fifth wife, was imprisoned and beheaded in the Tower, also on grounds of infidelity.

Elizabeth I spent time as a prisoner of the Tower during the reign of her older half-sister, Queen Mary. In 1553, Lady Jane Grey was imprisoned and executed in the Tower. She was placed on the throne for nine days following the death of the young King Edward VI by protestant nobles, who did not want the Catholic Princess Mary to rule the country.

However, Mary took over the throne and had Lady Jane Grey beheaded. Sir Walter Raleigh, a famous sea captain and former favorite of Queen Elizabeth, spent 13 years in the Tower. He was ultimately executed there.

In 1605 Guy Fawkes and his fellow conspirators were held and tortured in the Tower before facing execution for trying to blow up the King, his ministers, and the Houses of Parliament. William Penn, a member of Parliament and founder of Pennsylvania, was held for a time in the Tower. Henry Laurens, a former president of the American Continental Congress and Representative from South Carolina, was captured by the English on a trip to Holland and held in the Tower from 1779 until the end of the American Revolutionary War in 1781.

During World War I, the Tower held eleven prisoners convicted of being war spies. After World War II, Rudolf Hess, Deputy Fuhrer of Nazi Germany, was held in the Tower. He was its last prisoner.

Some prisoners were tortured in order to obtain information or confessions. There are two gruesome but fascinating displays of torture tools in the Tower. One is in the **Spanish Armoury** of the White Tower. The other is in the **Lower Wakefield Tower**, where interactive displays give you all the details. Ghost-busters claim that the cries of tortured prisoners can still be heard within the Tower's walls.

Most of the Tower's condemned prisoners were executed before a mob on Tower Hill. The luckier ones were beheaded with an ax. Other forms of execution involved hanging, being drawn (pulled apart by horses), or being quartered (disemboweled and cut into pieces). Only a privileged few were killed within the privacy of the Tower's walls. A plaque in the **Tower Green** marks the spot where Anne Boleyn and Catherine Howard lost their heads. Boleyn supposedly requested a sword rather than an ax for her execution – wisely believing that it was more likely to succeed with just one blow.

More than 2,000 of the Tower's prisoners were executed. Many of their remains are buried in the Tower's **Chapel of Saint Peter ad Vincula**.

Tower Ghosts. If transparent specters appear before you during your visit, don't be too surprised. The Tower of London is said to be filled with ghosts. Anne Boleyn and Lady Jane Grey are among those most commonly sighted wandering on the Tower Green. The Countess of Salisbury, beheaded by Henry VIII, was said to have faced execution kicking and screaming and still makes appearances that way. The ghost of King Henry VI, who was stabbed to death as he knelt in prayer, is said to haunt the Wakefield Tower. The two young princes, smothered in their sleep on orders of their uncle Richard III, are said to appear hand in hand in their night clothes. The ghost of Thomas Beckett, who was murdered in Canterbury Cathedral, is said to have made an appearance at the Tower when a new wing was under construction in 1241 – supposedly causing the new walls to collapse. There is even a ghost of a bear that was once part of the Tower's menagerie.

The **Crown Jewels** are in the Tower's Jewel House, which is part of the Waterloo Barracks. The collection is quite dazzling. There is a royal scepter fitted with the world's largest cut diamond – a 520-carat jewel known as the Star of Africa. There is a Royal punchbowl that's nearly as big as a bathtub. There are numerous royal crowns, including the Saint Edward Crown, used for royal ceremonies; the Queen Mother's Crown, which holds a diamond said to bring power to women and misfortune to men; and the Imperial State Crown designed for Queen Victoria in 1837 that contains 3,000 precious jewels (diamonds, pearls, sapphires, emeralds, rubies). Some of those jewels are very old, such as a ruby worn by King Henry V during the Battle of Agincourt, a sapphire worn by King Edward the Confessor, and a ruby that was given to the Black Prince by Pedro the Cruel of Castille.

In 1671, a gang of thieves led by a man named Captain Blood tried to make off with the Crown Jewels, which they stuffed into their clothing. They were discovered by the King's son, and captured following a dramatic chase within the Tower walls. The Jewel House Wardens are happy to tell you all about it and answer other questions. You can also visit the Crown and Diamonds exhibit, located in the Martin Tower, to learn more about the Royal Jewels.

Other sections of the Tower of London include the **Salt Tower**, where Jesuit prisoners were held – the walls still contain their etched inscriptions and symbols. The **Bell Tower** holds the bell that tolls when the Tower is closing for the evening. The **Traitors' Gate**, on the Thames side of the Tower complex, was the doorway through which prisoners were brought to the Tower by boat.

Huge **black ravens** live in the Tower grounds. Their wings are clipped so they cannot fly away – following a tradition that says if the ravens disappear the Tower will crumble and great disaster will befall the nation. A special Raven Master watches over the birds and can tell you each one's name. They eat a diet of raw meat and blood-soaked biscuits.

The Tower of London offers **special events and attractions** throughout the year. Many of these involved costumed guides and re-enactors who bring to life some of the mystery and intrigue of the Tower's history. There are also swordplay demonstrations, crafts fairs, daring escapes, and more.

During the Christmas holidays you can enjoy 12th century holiday food and entertainment. There are also Yeoman Warders' parades for Christmas and Easter.

When it's time to refuel there's a **New Armouries Café** in the Tower with hot and cold meals, kids' meals, sandwiches, and snacks. Outside the main entrance, there's the **Tower Café and Kiosk** that has grilled sandwiches, snacks, and ice cream. Otherwise, there's not much in the area, unless you head to St. Katherine's Warf or cross Tower Bridge and head towards Hays Galleria.

All Hallows By the Tower Church and Brass Rubbing Center. *Byward Street EC3. Tube: Tower of London. Open daily except Sun when services are held.*

The original church here was built in 675 AD on Roman pavements. It survived the Great Fire of 1666, even though the blaze started only a few streets away. William Penn (founder of Pennsylvania) was baptized here, and John Quincy Adams (6th US president) was married in this church in 1797. During World War II two bombs landed on All Hallows Church destroying all but the tower. It was rebuilt in 1957.

There is a **brass rubbing center** in the basement of the church – a fun activity for young and old.

Tower Bridge, *SE1. Tube: Tower Hill. Access to the bridge is free. Visit of the towers and exhibits called Tower Bridge Experience is open daily 10-6:30 (Apr-Oct); 9:30-6 (Nov-Mar). Adults: £7, Kids 5-15 yrs: £3, Family tickets available at various rates depending on family size, Kids under 5: free.*

Tower Bridge is one of the most recognized landmarks in all of London, and for many it really is *the* bridge that defines the city. Indeed, legend has it the wealthy American who bought London Bridge in the 1970s and moved it to Arizona actually thought he was getting this one. With its two towers and dual spans across the Thames, Tower Bridge truly is a beautiful piece of architecture.

Although its gothic style makes it look medieval, the Tower Bridge is actually relatively recent. It was built in 1894, with a steam-powered drawbridge that could be lifted to allow the passage of tall ships. If you are headed downstream, it is the last bridge that you will see across the Thames until you reach the English Channel.

Whether viewed from a tour boat or one of the river's banks, it is quite majestic. The two towers are 800 feet apart. You can walk through the towers from one side of the Thames to the other. If you start from the north side by the Tower of London, you can see the spot under the bridge, called Dead Man's Hole, where the bodies of drowning victims or people executed in the Tower sometimes were washed up and recovered in the old days.

To fully appreciate this structure, visit the **Tower Bridge Exhibition**. This tour takes you up the north tower, across the upper walkway (great views of the city from 60 feet up), and down into the south tower where you can see the bridge's original steam-powered engine room. Interactive exhibits will tell you about the bridge's history and explain how the drawbridge mechanism works. If your timing is right, you'll get to see it in action (now electrically powered) as it lifts open to let big ships through.

Saint Katharine's Dock. *St. Katharine's Way. East of the Tower Bridge on the N. Bank.*

This former shipping dock has been rebuilt with modern hotels, luxury apartments, offices, and shops. There is a marina that occasionally welcomes fancy yachts. It is a good place to catch a bite after visiting the Tower or Tower Bridge.

5. TRAFALGAR SQUARE

This square celebrates Britain's heroic past. However, with its large pedestrian esplanade, vibrant museums, constant traffic, and busy St. Martin in the Fields Church, Trafalgar Square is also a reflection of contemporary London's energy and diversity.

Trafalgar Square, *WC2, Tube: Charing Cross.*

This is London's most famous square, built from 1829 to 1841 to commemorate **Admiral Horatio Nelson**'s 1805 victory over Napoleon at Cape Trafalgar, off the coast of Spain. Nelson was a famous naval hero. Starting as a sailor at age 12, he rose to the rank of admiral by the age of 39. He won numerous important victories, but was severely injured in the process: he lost an eye in a 1794 battle and an arm in 1797. Nelson was mortally wounded in the Battle of Trafalgar but is immortalized here in a huge statue that stands atop a 165-foot column. The statue is 17 feet tall, even though in real life Admiral Nelson was only 5'4" tall. Every year on October 21, there is a solemn service below the column to honor him. At the base of the column, you can admire (and climb onto) four giant lion sculptures. Added to the monument in 1868, they were made from bronze obtained by melting down cannons from captured battle ships.

The **birds** of Trafalgar Square are a familiar and ancient tradition. In medieval days, the kings kept their hawks, falcons, and other birds of prey

here for hunting. For many years, tourists could buy bags of crumbs to feed the pigeons, but the mayor eventually banned the practice, declaring the birds to be a public nuisance and constant threat to the square's sculptures and buildings. Now, there's actually a stiff fine for fine for anyone caught feeding the pigeons. At one point, the city tried to drive away the pigeons by introducing falcons, their natural predators. The urbanized pigeons were no match for these foes, and the result was such a massacre it created a public outcry. Today, the remaining pigeons still provide good photo opportunities, and small children won't be able to resist chasing after them.

Each year in December, a giant **Christmas tree** is erected on Trafalgar Square. It comes as a gift from Norway in recognition Britain's help protecting the Norwegian Royal Family and fighting the Nazis during World War II. Carolers gather in the evenings to celebrate the season with songs. **New Year's Eve** is also celebrated here on Trafalgar Square. People come to hear Big Ben ring the twelve strokes of midnight. There is a big street party afterwards that inevitably results in drunken revelers jumping into the frigidly cold fountains.

The **National Gallery** is on the north side of Trafalgar Square. It is filled with paintings by great artists (see below). On the outside of the building, you can check out the **Imperial Standards of Length** etched into the stone under the balustrade. They show the official measures for 1 foot, 2 feet, and 1 yard. The **National Portrait Gallery** is next-door and contains portraits of famous Brits (see below).

The building on the east side of the Square is called the **South Africa House**. Check out the animal carvings on the stone arches. On the west side you can see the **Canada House**, where Canadian nationals can go look at their hometown newspapers, send email correspondences, or surf the web.

Notice that near the South Africa House there is a hollow pillar that looks like a street lamp and is just large enough for one person to stand inside. Look closely and you'll see a door and tiny windows. This pillar was built as a police observation post and is London's **tiniest police station**. It was mainly used to keep an eye on demonstrations – with a direct phone line to Scotland Yard. Since the 1960s it has been used as a place to store street cleaning equipment. The lantern on the top is said to come from one of Admiral Nelson's ships.

On the south side of Trafalgar Square facing Whitehall there is a **statue of King Charles I riding a horse**. It marks the spot from which all distances to London are measured. It is thus literally the **center of London**. Another equestrian statue on Trafalgar Square depicts King George IV riding bareback and dressed in Roman clothes. On the western side of the Square, facing the Mall, there is a triumphal arch called **Admiralty's Arch**.

Just SE of Trafalgar Square at 36 Craven Street is a house where **Benjamin Franklin** lived with his son William from 1757 to 1762.

Franklin was in England to represent the Pennsylvania Assembly. He had a great time there, living well and frequenting fellow writers, scientists, and philosophers. He was given an honorary Doctor of Law degree from Oxford University. Franklin loved whiling away late hours in heated political discussion at local coffee houses. He returned to the American colonies in 1762, but was quickly sent back to England (and to his Craven Street lodgings) to protest the British Stamp Act (a new form of tax on the colonies) for the Pennsylvania Assembly. By 1770, Franklin was also the official representative of New Jersey and Massachusetts. He regularly met with other American representatives: the Lee brothers of Virginia, Henry Laurens of South Carolina (who spent nearly 2 years in the Tower of London for standing up to the English), and John Boylston of Boston. The Thatched House Tavern on Saint James' Street became their official meeting place.

In 1766, Benjamin Franklin delivered an eloquent speech before Parliament calling for the repeal of the Stamp Act. By 1775, the battle for American Independence had begun in earnest. Franklin returned to Pennsylvania. His son, however, remained loyal to England, causing a painful falling out between the two of them.

Trafalgar Day Parade. *On Trafalgar Square, each year on the Sunday closest to October 21.*

This parade commemorates Admiral Nelson's victory on 21 October 1805 against Napoleon's forces in the Battle of Trafalgar. It features 500 naval cadets, marching bands, and all the proper pomp and circumstance. At the end a wreath is laid at the foot of Nelson's Column in Trafalgar Square.

National Gallery, *Trafalgar Square , WC2, Tube Charing Cross, Open daily, 10-6 (until 9 on Fri-Sat). Admission is free. Guided tours are offered at 11:30 and 2:30. You can design your own tour map in the computer room. Excellent audioguides let you hear about nearly any chosen piece in the museum. They are available for £3.50.*

Note: This museum goes out of its way to be **kid-friendly!** A **Museum Monster Hunt activity book** is available at the entrance for a small fee. There are **Kids' audio guides** with titles like "Royal Close-ups!," "Sensational Stories!," "Tell me a Picture," and more that are filled with humor and information. A **special kids' map** illustrated by Quentin Blake leads children ages 7-11 through the museum in the company of 2 secret agents who help them decode 20 of the Gallery's more popular paintings. Computer savvy kids can go on-line to the museum website (www.nationalgallery.org.uk) in the computer room to **tailor their own** museum tour map. The museum offers **other family-friendly activities** such as special talks, tours, theatrical presentations, costumed activities, arts and crafts, workshops and more. There are also good **kids' guides** in the museum bookshop, such as *Art Fraud Detective* by Nilsen that takes children through the museum following clues and a spot-the-difference game.

> ### Harry Potter Alert!
> Harry Potter fans take note: there is a hippogriff hiding in Room 41 of the National Gallery.

So, what's there to see? The National Gallery of London is one of the world's premier art museums. It contains Western European paintings spanning the years 1250 to 1900.

Thanks to all the museum's efforts to make its collections kid-friendly and accessible, this is really an excellent place to introduce your children to great paintings.

When it's time for a break there is a good café and an Italian restaurant, called Crivelli's Garden, with great views and selections such as panini and pizzas. High chairs are available.

By the way, outside, in front of the National Gallery, you'll see a bronze statue of George Washington – a gift from his home state of Virginia. After the American Revolution, Washington refused to ever set foot on British soil again, so the earth beneath the statue was transported from the United States.

National Portrait Gallery, *2 Saint Martin's Place, WC2, Tube: Leicester Square or Charing Cross. Open daily, 10-6 (until 9, Thurs-Fri). Admission: Free (although special exhibits may have a fee). CD audio-guide available in the Entrance Hall for a suggested donation of £3.*

Note: This museum is surprisingly **kid friendly!** For kids ages 3-12, the museum will lend you a **free activity backpack** filled with puzzles, dress-up items, objects to look for in the paintings, and more. Each pack contains eight different activities and they are available for the Tudor, Victorian, and 20th Century Galleries. Older kids and adults may enjoy using the museum's **CD Sound Guide** –a totally self-guided audio-tour.

So what is there to see? The National Portrait Gallery is dedicated to presenting portraits of notable British people, past and present. They also have temporary exhibits. Examples of people you may encounter in the permanent collection range from Beatrix Potter to Paul McCartney. There's also Chaucer, Shakespeare, Elizabeth I, Henry VIII, Nell Gwynne, the Brontë sisters, Lord Byron, Virginia Woolf, Princess Diana, Margaret Thatcher, Mick Jaggar, Joan Collins, and many more.

The paintings are displayed on transparent walls, giving the gallery space an open, airy feel. In other words, it's not the dusty or claustrophobic environment you might expect.

A few highlights:

- The museum's oldest portrait – it dates from 1505 and shows King Henry VII.
- The first portrait the museum ever acquired – of William Shakespeare, painted in 1610.
- The longest painting – called *Statesmen of WWI* (1924-1930) is 12 feet tall.
- The museum's widest portrait – 16 feet across, painted by John Singer Sargent in 1922, shows military officers from WWI.
- The smallest portrait – of Princess Henrietta Anne, painted in the 1600s, it is barely the size of a thumbnail.
- The skinniest portrait – depicts Rudyard Kipling and is nearly 4 times taller than it is wide.
- The squattest portrait – dates from the 1500s, portrays King Edward VI, and is 4 times wider than it is tall. It is a distorted image called an anamorphosis and needs to be viewed through a special device.
- The one with the most people in it - called The House of Commons (1833)
- The people with the most portraits in the museum – William Gladstone (former Prime Minister) has 65 portraits, Queen Elizabeth II has 50.

The museum's **Portrait Restaurant** offers fine food and spectacular rooftop views of London.

Have Your Portrait Done

Would you like to have your own portrait done? If so, there are two alternatives. The most popular is to head over the Leicester Square, where numerous artists will offer to do your caricature. You can also try heading down Charing Cross Road to a small park where local art students sometimes offer to draw portraits and caricatures. You won't get the quality of a da Vinci, but you will get a fun souvenir. Just be sure to agree on the price ahead of time.

It is a quite fancy and expensive, however. A less formal alternative is the **Portrait Café** located in the vaulted space of the lower level.

St. Martin-in-the-Fields Church, *Trafalgar Square, London WC2. Tube: Charing Cross. Free lunchtime concerts on Mon-Tues-Fri at 1pm.*

In the early 1200s, Saint Martin's was a church surrounded by fields that were used by the monks at Westminster. In 1542, King Henry VIII extended the church and its parish boundaries as an added buffer zone between his palace and city dwellers struck by the plague. In 1666, St. Martin in the Fields Church was one of the few structures to survive the Great London Fire. However, by 1721 it had fallen victim to changing styles. The old church was torn down and replaced with the one we see today, designed by architect James Gibbs (an admirer of Christopher Wren). When it was completed, the new Saint Martin in the Fields was widely considered an eyesore. However, it eventually became a model for churches worldwide, especially in the Northeastern United States.

Over the years, St. Martin-in-the-Fields has become well known for its open-door policy. It is the final resting place for the Nell Gwynn (notorious actress turned mistress of Charles II) as well as a highwayman named Jack Sheppard. It has a long history of helping the poor and feeding the hungry, and since 1964 Saint Martin in the Fields has welcomed a Chinese congregation that adds diversity to the church and its community.

The church is also highly renowned for the world-class quality of its **music**. You may have heard recordings by the Academy of St. Martin-in-the-Fields on your local classical radio station. The choir is also well regarded, the acoustics are great, and the church features many concerts by promising young artists from the London Music Conservatory. For a real treat, try to catch one of the **free lunchtime concerts** held every Mon-Tues-Fri at 1pm. There are also **evening, candlelight performances** that feature classical and baroque music by the greats, such as Mozart and Handel – who once performed here themselves. Tickets for the evening performances can be obtained at the box office (*Tel. 7839 8362*) or online.

Café in the Crypt, *St. Martins-in-the-Fields Church. Trafalgar Square, London WC2. Tube: Charing Cross. Open Mon-Sat 10-6; Sun 12-6.*

This is a great place to go with hungry kids. The food is good, and because it's served cafeteria-style you see what you're getting and don't have to wait to be served. You can get a drink, snack, or full meal with choices varied enough to fit most tastes. Although you are in a crypt and sitting on tombstones underfoot, the lit vaulted ceilings and large space make it seem quite airy.

The London Brass Rubbing Center, *St. Martin-in-the-Fields Church, Trafalgar Square, London WC2. Tube: Charing Cross. Open Mon-Sat 10-6; Sun 12-6. Admission is free, although you pay for brass rubbing supplies. The price varies according to the size of the rubbing.*

This is a fun activity with kids ages 7 and up. The Center offers 90 replicas of church brasses that include lords, ladies, kings, and queens as well as wonderful medieval creatures such as griffins, unicorns, and dragons. Additional choices include astrological and Celtic symbols, animals, armor, and historical figures such as William Shakespeare. The replicas are based on brass portraits contained in medieval churches all across England (there are some 7,000 in all). Many churches no longer let people make rubbings on the real portraits, or only do so with special permission, because it wears them down. However, even the replicas offer a unique glimpse of the clothing, armor, heraldry, and legends of Britain's past.

Once you've picked the image you want to use, staff from the Center will help you set up the paper and show you how to use the wax crayons. It takes some patience (so you may want to encourage that younger children pick a small one), but the end result is a cool souvenir that you've made yourself.

Note: If you don't have time to make a rubbing, you can purchase a kit to take home that is especially designed for kids. You can also buy a finished rubbing at the **gift shop**. The shop also has miniature brasses, knights, Celtic jewelry and other interesting souvenirs. In addition, there is a small crafts shop tucked in the back of the crypt that also offers interesting buys.

St. Martin-in-the-Fields Outdoor Market. *Located on the N. side of the church. Trafalgar Square. Tube: Charing Cross. Open Mon-Sat 11-5; Sun 12-5.*

This is a fun market with lots of clothes and crafts imported from India and South America. There are also sports team paraphernalia and souvenirs.

Charing Cross Road. *Trafalgar Square to Leicester Square and Cambridge Circus.*

The **Charing Cross** (across from the Charing Cross tube station) is a gothic-style funeral monument (*see photo on next page*) that was erected by King Edward I in 1290. It was one of a series of crosses he built to mark each spot in London where the funeral procession for his wife, Eleanor, stopped on its way to Westminster Abbey. It originally stood closer to Trafalgar Square, but was removed during the English Civil War. The one you see today is actually a replica of the original.

Charing Cross Road is most famous for its new and used **bookshops**. Charing Cross Road is also home to the **sculptures** of 18 famous historians and artists. The sculptor, Frederick Thomas, got his models from portraits in the National Portrait Gallery.

6. COVENT GARDEN/ SOMERSET HOUSE

Fans of the show *My Fair Lady* will remember that Covent Garden is where the flower girl with a thick Cockney accent named Eliza Dolittle is first discovered by Professor Henry Higgins, who transforms her into a fancy lady. While the flower and food stalls have largely disappeared from Covent Garden, its liveliness remains intact. Today, Covent Garden is a fun place to go to watch street entertainers, buy some souvenirs, grab a bite, or explore kid-friendly museums.

Somerset House has a more illustrious past and served as a residence to royalty. However, like Covent Garden, it is filled with interesting things to see and do.

Covent Garden. *Covent Garden Piazza, London WC2. Tube: Covent Garden, Leicester Square, or Temple.*

This area is named for a former *Convent* Garden of the Abbey of Saint Paul at Westminster. In the 1650s, it became home to the city's main market, housed in beautiful steel and glass structures. The market was moved to Battersea in the 1970s, though you can still see the market rules posted on the walls. Today Covent Garden features a vast array of shops and restaurants. There's a Punch and Judy puppet show, several old-fashioned toy stores, and interesting shopping for older kids. There are plenty of good eateries for meals or snacks, too, and a wide variety of street entertainers in the open spaces inside and out.

There are lots of interesting shops in the streets around Covent Garden, too. Heading north towards the tube station, you come to the lively **Neal Street**, filled with stores and restaurants. Nearby **Neal's Yard** has tempting cafés and bakeries, where everything is organic and vegetarian.

London Transport Museum. *Covent Garden Piazza, London WC2. Tube: Covent Garden, or Charing Cross. Open daily 10-7 (Fri 11-7;Sun 10-6). Adults: £10. Students: £8. Kids under 16 w/ and adult: free.*

Note: Ask about **special kid- and family-friendly activities**. This is a fun museum that's popular with kids and adults alike. It is housed in the former flower market building of Covent Garden. Appropriately enough for a Transport Museum, the building looks like a Victorian-era train station. Exhibits take you through the historical development of London's public transportation system, with lots of hands-on activities to keep kids engaged. You can try piloting a Tube train, a tram, a bus, or a signal system. You can be a station announcer, crawl through a life-size subway tunnel, or admire the inside of a plush train compartment. There are lots of double-decker vehicles – horse-drawn, electric, and diesel. Actors in period costumes answer questions and tell stories. Interactive computer displays offer information in multiple languages.

Doc Marten's Store. *17-19 Neal Street, Covent Garden. WC2. Tube: Covent Garden.*

For fans of Doc Marten's shoes and accessories this is the place to come. Depending on the exchange rate, they are generally cheaper here than in the States.

Tintin Shop. *34 Floral Street, W1. Tube: Covent Garden.*

Fans of this Belgian comic book series featuring the adventures of reporter Tintin, his loyal dog Snowy, and sea captain pal Captain Haddock will get a kick out of this store. It is filled with Tintin paraphernalia.

The Tea House. *15a Neal Street, WC2. Tube: Covent Garden.*

This shop is filled with interesting tea cups, tea pots, tea tins, and teas from all over the world. It's a great gift-buying opportunity, located in a lively street running north of Covent Garden Market.

St. Paul's Church. *Bedford Street, WC2. On the Piazza in front of Covent Garden. Tube: Covent Garden.*

This church (not to be confused with St. Paul's Cathedral) is known as the Actors' Church. Inside are memorials to famous actors and play-wrights.

In May there is a puppet festival in the church garden, celebrating Punch and Judy, with free puppet shows.

Twinings Tea Shop. *216 The Strand, WC2. Tube: Charing Cross.*

Located just south of Covent Garden Market, this is a great address for teas and tea accessories.

Somerset House, *The Strand, WC2. Tube: Charing Cross, Temple, Embankment, or Holborn. Open daily 10-6. Entrance: free.*

Somerset House was a former palace for the Duke of Somerset and now offers a wide variety of activities, ranging from exhibits and concerts to an ice-skating rink that is open from late November through January.

Courtauld Gallery. *Somerset House. Open daily 10-6. Adults £5, Kids under 18 free. Free to all on Mondays before 2pm.*

The Courtauld Gallery contains works by old Masters, Impressionists, and Post-Impressionist painters. Kids may enjoy it more than you think, like the cartoonish quality of medieval works, ballerinas by Degas, or gory story of how Vincent Van Gogh cut off his own ear in an epileptic fit, pictured in his *Self-Portrait with Bandaged Ear* (*photo below*).

7. THE WEST END

PICCADILLY, OXFORD, & BOND STREETS
Leicester Square

This area is most well known for being the center of London's theater and movie scene. It's also a great place to go window shopping with everything from classic British department stores to trendy fashions. Or come here to grab a meal – whether it's a picnic from the outdoor street market, dim sum in Chinatown, or a hamburger at the Rainforest Café.

Piccadilly Circus. *W1. At the convergence of Piccadilly, Regent Street, Shaftesbury Avenue, Haymarket, and Coventry Street. Tube: Piccadilly Circus.*

Piccadilly Circus is the London equivalent of New York's Times Square. It is in the heart of London's Theater District.

In the middle of Piccadilly Circus stands a monument to the Victorian philanthropist, Lord Shaftesbury. Erected in 1893, it is supposed to depict the Angel of Christian Charity.

However, most people will tell you that it depicts Eros, the Greek god of love. The statue was the first in London to be made of aluminum. When the monument was built, it also included a drinking fountain with a public drinking cup, but they've disappeared.

Regent Street, which connects Piccadilly Circus to Oxford Circus and Pall Mall, is known for its classic high-end shopping. Going west from Piccadilly Circus is a glass-roofed shopping gallery called **Burlington Arcade**, which is still patrolled by police in top hats and livery known as "Beadles." They help keep up the standards and maintain order, including rules against "whistling, singing, and hurrying." At #197 Piccadilly, there is a market where crafts and antiques are sold Tues, Wed, Sat in front of **St. James Church**. Inside the church is a place to make brass rubbings. There are occasionally free lunchtime concerts.

New Bond, Old Bond, and **Oxford Streets** also feature high-end shopping; there are traditional British names like Burberry, Selfridges, and Marks & Spencer as well as names from Milan, Paris, and New York.

Leicester Square. WC2. Tube: Leicester Square.

Leicester Square is a lively spot, smack in the middle of London's theater district. But the shows aren't just on the stage here. The Square has plenty of live street entertainment in the form of jugglers, musicians, and other performers. There are also several movie theaters for those who prefer to watch the action on the big screen. These are especially big, boasted to be some of the largest movie screens in London, though the tickets are said to be some of the most expensive, too.

While the movies may be pricier here than in other parts of town, if you want **bargain theater tickets** this is the place to come. Although several booths advertise discounted tickets, the official one is called **TKTS** and is run by the Society of London Theaters. It is located in the clocktower building on the south side of the square, and it offers reduced-price tickets for that day's performances (open Mon-Fri 10-7, Sun noon-3). You can save as much as 50% off the regular price, even though there is a small processing fee. Bring cash because they don't take credit cards. Beware of other vendors that advertise discounted tickets but don't always deliver on the promise.

There are two important tributes to the performing arts here in Leicester Square. One is the statue of **Charlie Chaplin**, dressed as his famous character, The Tramp. In case your kids have never heard of him you can remind them that Chaplin (1889-1977) was a famous movie actor and director. He is most well known for his comic, silent movie roles. Thanks to his theatrical talent, he was able to rescue himself and his brother from a childhood spent in an orphanage for destitute children. Chaplin made over 80 films. Some of the most well-known include *The Tramp, The Kid, The Great Dictator*, and *Modern Times*. The other theater tribute here is a replica of the monument to **William Shakespeare** that stands in Westminster Abbey.

You can also see a bust of painter **William Hogarth**, famous for drawing caricatures, and one of **Isaac Newton**. Both of them lived in the neighborhood. Hogarth's influence lives on in Leicester Square – there are any number of artists who will offer to **draw your caricature**, for a fee. Just make sure to settle on the price in advance.

Chinatown, Gerrard Street. *Just south of Shaftesbury Avenue. Tube: Piccadilly or Leicester Square.*

Though small, London's Chinatown is filled with good Chinese restaurants.

Berwick Street Market. *London W1. Tube: Piccadilly Circus or Leicester Sq. Open Mon-Sat 9-5.*

This colorful market features fresh produce, cheese, bread, herbs, and household goods. Berwick Street also has fun shops.

8. BUCKINGHAM PALACE

Buckingham Palace. *Buckingham Palace Road, SWI. Tube: Green Park, St. James' Park, or Victoria Station. Visits to the Palace State Rooms offered daily in August and September, 10-6. Price (includes audio guide): Adults: £17. Students/over 60:£15.50. Under 17: £9.75. Under 5: Free. Family: £45 (2 adults, 3 under 17s). Tickets are distributed daily starting at 9 for specific times. You can save time by purchasing tickets in advance online at www.royal.gov.uk or via phone: 20 7766 7300. You can also buy a combined ticket for the State Rooms, Royal Mews, and Queen's Gallery.*

Buckingham Palace houses the royal family, their offices, and their staff. It is the center of royal business and many state visits. More than 50,000 guests are received at the Palace each year for royal banquets, lunches, dinners, garden parties, and receptions. There are 775 rooms.

Tourists are allowed to visit the State Rooms and Throne Room only when the Queen takes her summer holiday in August and September. The Rooms are decorated with lavish furnishings, fine porcelains, and artistic masterpieces by Rembrandt, Rubens, Vermeer, Poussin, and Canaletto. Special displays show off historical fashions, musical instruments, manuscripts, photographs, and souvenirs. The audio tour includes voices and music of the past.

By the way, do you know how to tell whether the Queen is at home? When she is in residence, there are four sentry guards in front of Buckingham Palace. When she is away there are only two. You can tell which regiment is guarding the palace by the plumes on their bearskin hats: red=Coldstreams, white=Grenadiers, blue=Irish Guards, white and green=Welsh Guards, no plume=Scottish Guards.

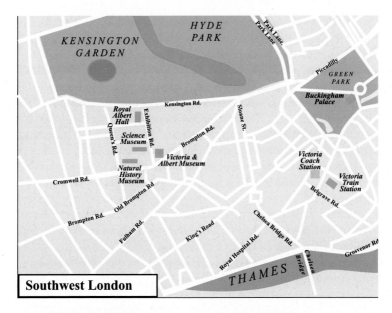

Southwest London

Memorial to Queen Victoria. *In front of Buckingham Palace, at the beginning of the Mall.*

Queen Victoria ruled from 1837 to 1901 over one of the largest empires in history. This memorial was commissioned by her son, Edward VII. It is said to be the largest royal monument in England, although the one built for Prince Albert in Hyde Park is a close competitor. This memorial took five years to complete and required 2,300 tons of marble. It's a good spot from which to view the Changing of the Guard.

Changing of the Guard. *Buckingham Palace Road. Daily at 11:30, Apr-Aug. Every other day from Sept-Mar. See photo on page 55.*

> *They're changing the guard at Buckingham Palace —*
> *Christopher Robin went down with Alice.*
> *Alice is marrying one of the guard.*
> *"A soldier's life is very hard,"*
> *Says Alice.*
> —When We Were Very Young, A.A. Milne

It's hard to resist the temptation of following in the footsteps of Christopher Robin to see the changing of the Guard at Buckingham Palace. It's one of the most colorful and traditional sites in London, filled with royal pageantry.

Here's how it works: The new guards arrive at Buckingham Palace at 11:30 in the morning, marching from Wellington Barracks, which are located on Birdcage Walk along the south side of St. James Park. They process into the palace gates where they are reviewed as the military band plays on. The music varies considerably. You may get something along the lines of *Rule Brittania*, but more likely it will be something modern. We heard *New York, New York* and *Springtime in Paris*. This lasts about 30 minutes, after which the guard members who are going off duty march out of the gates and back toward the Wellington Barracks.

If you go during high tourist season, the long wait and large crowds by the palace can be a bit much for smaller children, so here are some survival strategies:

Option 1. Arrive early and find a place to sit on the Victoria Monument or along the Buckingham Palace gates. If you arrive by 11, you can watch the guards go through their inspection.

Option 2. Arrive late (at noon) and watch the end of the procession along Birdcage Walk (the road that runs along St. James Park) as the relieved guards return to the Wellington Barracks. We didn't arrive until 11:30 on a hot, crowded day, but were lucky to find a spot seated across from the Palace gates in front of the Queen Victoria Memorial. We couldn't see what was happening within the gates but had a front row view as they marched out.

Wellington Barracks. *Birdcage Walk, SW1. Tube: Victoria Station.*

This is where the Royal Palace Guards retire after the Changing of the Guard. If you catch them at the end of the ceremony you will be able to watch them go off duty and take on a much more relaxed attitude. There is an interesting gift shop just to the right of the Barracks entrance that sells collectors' miniatures of soldiers and royal scenes. The items are pricey, but the displays are worth a look.

By the way, Birdcage Walk, along St. James Park is named for the fact that it was once a Royal Aviary.

Royal Mews. *5 Buckingham Gate, SW1. Tube: Victoria Station. Open daily 10-5 (Jul-Sep) and daily except Fri 11-4 (Mar-Jul; Oct) Closed Nov-Feb. Adults: £7.75. Students: £ 7. Children 5-17:£5. Kids under 5: free. Family (2 adults and 3 kids): £20.50. You can purchase tickets in advance at www.royal.gov.uk or phone: 020 7766 7302.*

Note: Special family-friendly activities are organized at the Mews during weekends and holidays. These include arts and crafts, storytelling, and descriptions of all the decorations and symbols associated with Royal transportation.

This is where the Royal Carriages and Cars are kept and maintained. It includes a working stable where you can see some of the Windsor Grey and Cleveland Bay horses trained to deal with the noise and bustle of Palace life. There are also all the vehicles, horse drawn and motorized, that transport the royal family to important Royal events. Examples include the Glass Coach used for weddings, the Irish State Coach that the Queen takes to open sessions of Parliament, and the Gold State Coach used for coronations – so loaded with gold leaf and decorations that it weighs nearly 4 tons and requires 8 horses to pull. There's also a selection of Rolls Royces.

The Mall. *SW1.*

This grand avenue links Buckingham Palace to Trafalgar Square. It was laid out during the reign of King Charles II along St. James Park. It is the scene of many royal processions; and when foreign dignitaries are in town, it is lined with their national flags. You won't find the sort of shopping American kids might expect from a Mall, but you will find open air stands along St. James Park that sell books, posters, arts/crafts, and souvenirs.

9. WHITEHALL

This large avenue gets its name from the enormous Whitehall Palace that once stood along the Thames here and was the primary residence of the Stuart monarchs. Today, it encompasses some of London's most important political addresses, including the Prime Minister's residence and government offices.

Changing of the Horse Guard. *Between Horse Guard Road by St. James Park and Whitehall. SWI. Tube Charing Cross or Westminster. Daily at 11 (noon on Sun). Guard review daily at 4. Admission: free.*

Little is left of Whitehall Palace (only the Banqueting House across the avenue) but there are still mounted horse guards keeping watch. Their sentry boxes are located along Whitehall and provide fabulous photo opportunities. Although the guards won't flinch, they will let you approach for a family snapshot. By the way, there are actually two groups of mounted guards that take turns watching over Whitehall. The Life Guards wear red tunics and have white plumes in their helmets. The Blues & Royals wear blue tunics and have red plumes.

Fresh horses are brought out every hour, but the formal changing of the horse guard takes place each morning at 11 (10 on Sundays). The replacement guards leave their barracks in Hyde Park at 10:30 and make their way through Green Park and St. James Park to the wide court behind Whitehall called Horse Guards Parade. They pass through the archways to the Whitehall side. The horses are beautiful and it's a good show to see with

kids. There's plenty of room to watch, and once the 30-minute ceremony is complete, you are allowed to pet the horses and have your photo taken next to them. If you miss the morning show there is another ceremony at 4, when the horse guards are reviewed and inspected. **Kids take note:** The area called Horse Guards Parade used to be where the Whitehall Palace knights held their jousting tournaments.

In mid-June there is a special ceremony called the **Trooping of the Color,** when the Royal Guards process before the Queen to mark the so-called, official royal birthday. It's nowhere near the day of Queen Elizabeth's birth, but that's tradition for you. The event dates back to 1755, when the army colors (flags) were displayed in front of the soldiers so that they would recognize them in battle. Today, the colors are trooped before the Queen on the esplanade of Horse Guards Parade. Then they follow her down the Mall to Buckingham Palace. Six guard units participate in this event, including five units of foot guards (Grenadiers, Coldstreams, Scots, Irish, and Welsh) and one unit of cavalry. There are hundreds of musicians and plenty of pomp and circumstance.

During the first two weeks of June, you can watch the guards **beat the retreat** from Whitehall several evenings a week. It is a sort of dress rehearsal for the Trooping of the Colors.

Speaking of colors, note how Whitehall is lined with fences topped with arrowheads. These were originally painted in bright colors. However, when Queen Victoria's husband died, she ordered that they all be painted black, and they've stayed that way ever since.

Old Scotland Yard. *Corner of Whitehall and Great Scotland Yard, near Trafalgar Square. Note: although you can't visit the inside, it's fun to know the history of this famous building.*

Scotland Yard is the headquarters of the London Metropolitan Police. It was originally housed here and named for a palace built in the 12th century that was used as a residence by visiting Scottish kings. It was moved in 1829 to a new local along the Thames embankment, by Westminster Bridge which became known as New Scotland Yard. New Scotland Yard was moved once again in 1967 to its present location on Victoria Street near the St. James Park tube station.

The Old Scotland Yard building once contained a collection of criminal relics called the Black Museum. It displayed tools, weapons, and forgeries used by criminals from famous trials, as well as death masks of prisoners hanged in the Newgate Prison. Like many historic London locales, it was said to be haunted by ghosts.

By the way, did you know that London's police officers are called "Bobbies" – a name that comes from the fact that the modern (19th century) police force was created by a man whose name was Sir Robert Peel. Other nicknames have included "Peelers" (again for Sir Robert) and

"Charlies" (a name given to nightwatchmen in the 18th century). Bobbies are easy to identify with their black uniforms and elongated black helmets. They do not carry firearms (except at airports, nuclear facilities, in Northern Ireland, and on protection duties). They do carry a night stick (called a baton in England) and pepper spray.

Cabinet War Rooms. *Clive Steps, King Charles Street, SW1. (Just S. of the Horse Guards) Tube: Westminster or St James's Park. Open daily 9:30-6. Adults £15; Kids 15 and under: Free.*

Note: Kids are fascinated by this visit, which has a free **audioguide** including special versions for kids. Also ask for the **Family Trail Activity Sheet** available at the audioguide desk.

The Cabinet War Rooms were developed in 1938 (and opened one week before World War II broke out) as a place to protect the Prime Minister and his Cabinet from the threat of German bombs and gas attacks during World War II. Winston Churchill used this bunker throughout the duration of the war. Kept secret until 1981, the Rooms were set up in the basements of the Office of Works' Building – conveniently located between Parliament and the Prime Minister's house at #10 Downing on

Street. When the war officially ended in 1945, the Cabinet War Rooms were abandoned. They were left *as is* and remained undisturbed for years.

Now open to the public, the self-guided tour gives a real feel for the Spartan, bunker-like conditions in which top British officials lived and planned military strategies during long shifts in claustrophobic conditions. There are close-up views of underground and windowless bedrooms, offices, the typing pool, and the Churchills' kitchen and dining room. You see the Map Room with pins marking troop positions exactly as they were 16 August 1945; the Telephone Room with its color-coded phones; the BBC broadcast station; and the Cabinet Room where Churchill met with Ministers, military advisors, and Members of Parliament to discuss news and strategies.

After the tour, you can exchange your Family Trail activity sheet for a special War Rooms' Pass. Then it's a good idea to re-emerge above ground and enjoy the fresh air and natural beauties of St. James' Park, across the street.

Prime Minister's Residence. *#10 Downing Street. SW1. Just off Whitehall, near the Cabinet War Rooms. Tube: Westminster. Not accessible to visitors.*

You won't be able to get very close to the Prime Minister's Georgian-style townhouse, but you can get a glimpse of this famous address from either Whitehall or Horse Guards Road. For security reasons, the street is blocked off and guarded by both traditional policemen and more heavily armed special units.

Cenotaph. *In the middle of Parliament Street, between Parliament Square and Trafalgar Square. SW1. Tube: Westminster.*

A cenotaph is an empty tomb or monument in memory of someone who has died elsewhere. This cenotaph, which is shaped like an obelisk, pays tribute to all the members of the British Commonwealth who lost their lives in the First and Second World Wars. Each year, they are remembered on November 11 in a solemn ceremony that includes members of royal families, politicians, ambassadors, and military representatives from numerous countries. They attend a memorial service then come to lay wreaths of poppies on the monument.

Victoria Embankment. *Along the Thames, parallel to Whitehall. SW1. Tube: Westminster.*

There is a small park here and two piers (Westminster and Charing Cross) where you can catch boats to Greenwich and other spots along the Thames. There are numerous moored ships along the embankment, including the *Hispaniola* (a restaurant), *Tattershall Castle* (a paddlewheel steamer), a River Police boat, the St. Katherine, the HQS Wellington, and the HMS President.

Between Embankment and the Waterloo Bridge there is a 60-foot granite obelisk known as **Cleopatra's Needle**. It dates from 1475 BC and was given to Britain by a Turkish Viceroy in Egypt. The delivery of the gift was complicated by the fact that the obelisk weighs 186 tons and fell over during its transfer. It was many years before a British engineer figured out how to design a pontoon to carry it to the sea. The obelisk was nearly lost in a storm in the Bay of Biscay, but finally reached London in 1878. Numerous objects where placed under its base on the embankment, including coins, a newspaper of the day, a railway guide, bible, box of pins, and photos of the best looking English women of the day. If you look at the Needle closely, you can see shrapnel damage from World War I.

Also along the Victoria Embankment is a memorial to members of the Royal Navy who were lost in submarines during World War I. The names of those lost in World War II have also been added.

During the summer, there are numerous ethnic festivals along the Victoria Embankment celebrating the music and cultures of the world. Parades, like the Lord Mayor's Show parade pictured below, often pass along the Embankment.

Heading west along the Victoria Embankment is an area known as **The Temple**. It is named for the Templar Knights, a rich and powerful order founded in 1169, who had their London headquarters here. They were both knights and monks, and they were charged with protecting pilgrims in the Holy Land. They eventually fell into disfavor with the Pope, due to their wealth and influence. In the early 1300s they were accused of heresy and burned at the stake. **Temple Church** within the Temple complex dates back to the 12th century and is an example of Norman round church architecture. On Inner Temple Lane is a pillar called **Temple Bar**. Although it sounds the name for a pub, it's actually a boundary marker delineating a historic city limit and now bordering the center of London's financial life.

10. WESTMINSTER

WESTMINSTER, HOUSES OF PARLIAMENT,& TATE BRITAIN

You know you're really in London when you can spot the clock tower of Big Ben and hear its majestic tone. It tolls over an area rich with history – stories of kings and queens, traitors and heroes, poets and rowdy parliamentarians. There's much to see and explore here, just don't forget your camera!

Houses of Parliament. *Parliament Square, SW1. Tube: Westminster. Guided Tours are conducted in Aug-Sept, Mon-Sat from 9:30 to 4:15. They last 75 minutes. You must obtain tickets in advance at the special Ticket Office on Abingdon Green, opposite Parliament & The Victoria Tower Gardens; or online at www.ticketmaster.co.uk; or by phoning 0844 847 1672. Prices vary depending on time of year and whether you are UK nationals or not. Count on spending about Adults: £15, Students and Kids 5-16: £7, Family ticket: £35 (2 adults, 2 kids under 16), Kids under 5: free. Those assisting persons with disabilities: free. Note: Large bags are not allowed, and there is no place to store them.*

Note: Watching a session of Parliament or climbing up the Big Ben Tower is only allowed if you are a UK citizen, and you must obtain a ticket from your Member of Parliament. Non-UK citizens can visit the Commons and Lords Chamber's, the Queen's Robing Room, the Royal Gallery, and Westminster Hall.

The word parliament means "a place to talk" and the Houses of Parliament are no exception – plenty of talking and argument goes on within the great walls of

this building. The British Parliament is composed of the House of Commons (elected by the people), House of Lords (inherited through noble titles), and the Queen, who formally opens each annual session in November. The House of Commons proposes and votes on new laws. There are 659 Members of the House of Commons. The House of Lords only discusses or amends laws.

Sessions of Parliament have been held since the year 1275. The original Members met at Saint Stephens Chapel, where they sat on opposite sides of the central aisle, much as they do today. They began to meet in Westminster Palace when Henry VIII moved his household to Whitehall Palace in 1532.

During the night of November 4, 1605, Guy Fawkes, Robert Catesby, and other Catholic conspirators tried to blow up Westminster Palace, including both Houses of Parliament, King James I (a Protestant), and his ministers. Their plan, known as the Gunpowder Plot, was discovered ahead of time, however, and they were caught red-handed in the cellars of Westminster Palace. They were tried in Westminster Hall of the Houses of Parliament, and then taken to the Tower of London, where they were executed. Every year in November, **Guy Fawkes Day** is celebrated as a national holiday. Merry-makers set big bonfires and burn effigies of Guy Fawkes.

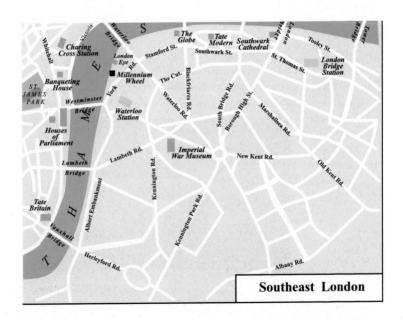

Southeast London

In 1834 a fire destroyed much of the Westminster Palace. Today, only Westminster Hall and the Jewel Tower remain from the original building. The Houses of Parliament were rebuilt in a magnificent gothic-revival-style. The resulting building is truly huge. There are 11 courtyards, 100 staircases, 1,100 rooms, and two miles of corridors. There are also 8 bars and 6 restaurants, but they are not open to the general public. The entire building covers 8 acres. The eastern façade stretches 940 feet along the Thames River.

Some of the most famous rooms within the Houses of Parliament include the House of Commons Chamber, destroyed by bombs in 1941 and later rebuilt; the Robing Room, where the queen puts on her crown and robe before officially opening Parliament each year; and Westminster Hall, with its magnificent hammerbeam roof, decorated with stars and angels. There is a plaque in the Hall commemorating William Wallace – the Scottish hero portrayed in by Mel Gibson the movie *Braveheart*.

Outside on the west side of the building there is an equestrian statue of **King Richard the Lionheart**, dressed in full armor, sword raised, and ready for battle. The pose is appropriate since Richard spent more time battling the French to maintain English holdings in Normandy or fighting in the Crusades, than he did ruling England.

Big Ben. *Northern side of the Houses of Parliament, Parliament Square, SW1. Tube: Westminster.*

This famous clock tower is one of London's most recognizable landmarks. It shows up in many classic children's films, such as Mary Poppins and Peter Pan. The tower, which is 316 feet tall, is actually called Saint Stephen's Tower. Big Ben is really the name of the enormous bell inside the tower that rings each hour. Some say that it was named for a famous heavy-weight boxing champion called Ben Caunt. More likely, Big Ben was named after Benjamin Hall, the city's first commissioner of public works (1855-1858) whose name is inscribed inside the bell. It weighs 13.8 tons.

The chimes that you hear every 15 minutes from the Parliament clock tower are called the Westminster Chimes. They are set to music by Handel, with words that go like this: "All through this hour, Lord be my Guide. And by thy power, no foot shall slide."

The clocks on the tower are illuminated when Parliament is in session. They are really quite huge. Each clock face is 23 feet wide. The minute hands are 14 feet long and the Roman numerals are 2 feet tall. The clock dates from 1859 and keeps nearly perfect time. Old coins are added or subtracted to the clock's 5-ton mechanism when small adjustments are needed. It is rewound automatically now, but before 1913 the clock was rewound by hand. It took 2 men 32 hours to wind it up all the way.

The large tower on the other end of the Houses of Parliament is called Victoria Tower. It houses a copy of every bill ever signed into law by Parliament, going back to the 1400s. If you can see the Union Jack (British flag) flying from this tower it means that the House of Commons is in session.

Westminster Abbey. *Broad Sanctuary, next to Parliament Square, SW1. Tube: St James's Park or Westminster. Open Mon-Fri 9:30-4:30 (until 6 on Wed); Sat 9:30-1:45. Open Sun for services. There is a fee to visit the Abbey. Adults: £15, kids 11-18: £6, Family ticket: £30-42, depending on number of people. Children under 11: free. Visitors in wheelchairs and their guides: free. Sunday religious services are open to all free of charge. Guided 1.5 hour tours are available for £3 per person. Audioguides, narrated by Jeremy Irons, are free with your entry ticket. There is a special "children's trail" available free of charge at the information desk.*

Westminster Abbey is considered both a House of God and House of Kings. It is a place of worship, the sight of Royal Coronations, and the final resting place for thousands of important historical figures. It is an Anglican Church, not to be confused with Westminster Cathedral, which is Roman Catholic.

The original abbey was built during reign of King Edward the Confessor, as an enlargement of a Benedictine monastery near his Palace of Westminster. It was consecrated in 1065 AD, just before Edward's death. In the 13th century, Westminster Abbey was rebuilt to emulate the great cathedrals that were being constructed in France and England. Outside you can see the magnificent flying buttresses that help support the weight of the walls and roof – 100 feet tall and the highest in all of Britain.

The first English king to be crowned in Westminster Abbey was Harold the Saxon in January 1066, who reigned less than a year. Harold was defeated by William of Normandy in the Battle of Hastings. The victor became known as William the Conqueror and was crowned as the new King of England in the Abbey on Christmas Day 1066. The tradition of Royal Coronations at Westminster has continued ever since.

The best way to approach a visit to Westminster Abbey with children is to look at is as a great scavenger hunt. Pick out a number of objects and memorials that you want to see ahead of time (there are over 3,000 in all), then make it a game to see who can spot them first. Or use the audioguide, which leads you through in about one hour. By the way, don't be discouraged by the fact that many of the tombs near the entrance of the tour are unmarked or belong to people you've never heard of. You'll get to the good stuff soon enough. Below are descriptions of many of the notable features and memorials in Westminster, to help you choose:

Shrine of Edward the Confessor. North Ambulatory, behind the Coronation Chair. This wooden structure contains Edward's ashes. You will only see a glimpse of it because it is fragile and protected from visitors.

Coronation Chair. Located behind the choir and before the Henry VII Chapel. This chair dates from the early 1300s and has been used for the coronation of every English king and queen since Edward II. One exception: when William III and Mary II were crowned as joint monarchs in 1689, a special chair, now in the Abbey Museum, was made for Mary. The Coronation Chair is made of oak and was constructed for King Edward I to contain the **Stone of Scone** – a legendary rock on which Irish and Scottish kings were crowned that the English stole from the Scots. (Note: after centuries of contention, it was recently returned to Scotland). The chair is decorated with birds, foliage, animals, and the figure of a king (either Edward I himself or Edward the Confessor) whose feet are resting on a lion. It is surprisingly small, considering its importance.

Tombs of Queen Elizabeth I, Mary Tudor (left alcove) and **Mary Queen of Scots,** (right alcove) in the Henry VII Chapel, also called the Lady Chapel.

Tombs of the princes Edward and Richard, also in Henry VII Chapel. These were the boys locked in the Tower of London and murdered by their uncle, who became King Richard III.

Also to be seen in the Henry VII Chapel are tombs of Henry VII and his mistress, Elizabeth of York. Note, too, the incredible English **Gothic ceilings**; the flags and crests of members of the **Knights of Malta**; stained glass window dedicated to the men of the **Royal Air Force**; and hole in the window covered with glass left over from German WWII **bomb damage**.

Scientists' Corner. Located in the center of the sanctuary with memorials to Sir Isaac Newton and Charles Darwin.

Poets' Corner, located in the South Transept, includes literary greats such as Geoffrey Chaucer, John Dryden, Alfred Lloyd Tennyson, Robert Browning, Samuel Johnson, Charles Dickens, Rudyard Kipling, Lewis Carroll, and Thomas Hardy. Also William Shakespeare, Lord Byron, John Milton, William Wordsworth, Thomas Gray, John Keats, Percy B. Shelley, Robert Burns, William Blake, T.S. Eliot, Jane Austen, the Brontë sisters, and Henry James. Shakespearean actors, David Garrick and Sir Laurence Olivier, and composers George Frederic Handel and Henry Purcell are here, too.

Politician's corner, in the North transept: Memorials to Prime Ministers William Pitt, William Gladstone, Disraeli, and many others.

High Altar. In the center of the Abbey. The area with the black and white paved floor is where coronations take place. It is also where the caskets of **Diana, Princess of Wales** and the **Queen Mother** were placed during their funerals.

Tomb of the Unknown Warrior. Located in the middle aisle of the nave (near the exit). A tribute to the many thousands of unidentified soldiers killed in World War I. There's also a US Congressional Medal of Honor on a nearby pillar that was placed on the unknown soldier's tomb, and memorials to both Winston Churchill and Franklin D. Roosevelt.

Cloisters. Look for tributes to astronomer Halley (of Halley's Comet) and Captain James Cook, the great explorer. The Abbey Cloisters also contain a **Brass Rubbing Center**, where you can make your own print from replicas of tomb portraits.

West entrance (used as the exit during the visit). Memorials to ten contemporary heroes, including Martin Luther King.

Abbey Museum, housed in the vaulted cellars that date back to the Norman foundations of the church. Contains wax effigies of Edward III, Henry VII, Elizabeth of York, Elizabeth I, Charles II, Admiral Nelson, William Pitt. Also copies of royal jewels used for coronation rehearsals, and other Royal clothes and arms.

The **College Garden** at Westminster Abbey occupies a site that has been under continuous cultivation for more than 900 years. The monks used it to grow food and medicinal plants. Today, the garden is still filled with beautiful plants, but it is no longer used to grow food because of a high lead content in the soil.

Outside, on the SE side of the Abbey, there is a small church called St. Margaret's. On the pavement nearby is a **Giant Sundial**. Kids can try to figure out the time and date using their own shadows.

Parliament Square on the north side of Westminster Abbey is decorated with statues of famous statesmen, including Winston Churchill, Abraham Lincoln, and others.

Westminster Bridge. *By Big Ben. Tube: Westminster.*

This graceful stone bridge connects the Houses of Parliament with the South Bank, including City Hall, the Aquarium, and Waterloo Station. It is 44 feet wide, 1,200 feet across and offers great views of Big Ben, the London Eye, and the Tower Bridge.

On the NW side of the bridge (by the Westminster tube stop) is a large statue of **Queen Boadicea**, head of a Celtic tribe called the Iceni. They were some of the local inhabitants of this area when the Romans invaded Britain in 55AD. They were known to worship trees, sacrifice virgins, and cover their bodies in blue war paint. Queen Boadicea led a revolt against the Roman invaders in 60 AD. She and her tribesmen successfully liberated Londinium and killed tens of thousands of Romans. Their triumph was short lived, however. The revolt was squashed and Boadicea and her family swallowed poison to avoid Roman capture. Legend has it that she is buried in a mound atop Parliament Hill in Hampstead Heath.

Tate Britain Museum. *Millbank, SW1. Tube: Pimlico, Vauxhall, or Westminster. Also accessible via the Tate Boat, which runs every 40 minutes with stops at the Tate Britain, London Eye, and Tate Modern. Open daily 10-6. Admission is free, but donations are welcome. Audioguides are available for £3.50. Check out the special family events at http://www.tate.org.uk/families/ events/britain/ There is also a kids' page at: http://kids.tate.org.uk/*

Note: This museum is full of activities for kids and families, including a **Secret Tate Discovery Trail** and **Art Trolley**, available in the galleries on weekends, packed with with games, trails and other fun stuff for families to do together. The museum also organizes other **family activities** on weekends and holidays. There are **babychanging facilities** in the restrooms by the Café and in near the Auditorium.

This museum features British art from 1500 to today (*see photo on next page*). The great classics are all here including Blake, Constable,

Gainsborough, Hogarth, Rossetti and the Pre-Raphaelites. There are modern works by Henry Moore, Francis Bacon, and Gilbert and George. There are entire galleries devoted to the magnificent landscape paintings of JMW Turner – these alone are worth the visit.

Although most kids would balk at the idea of enjoying an art museum, they end up having fun at this one thanks to the excellent kid-friendly resources the museum has to offer. Many of the paintings have a story to tell; and these are brought to life through the audioguides and activities that highlight tales of the bald queen, the man who hated red pantaloons, the soldier with bare legs, the ghost of a flea, and other humorous anecdotes.

M.I.5. Headquarters. *Milbank. (Across from the Tate Britain)*

Fans of spy movies take note. This building houses the headquarters of the counter-intelligence arm of the British Secret Service. Their role is to identify drug traffickers, foreign spies, and terrorists. You can't visit the building, but it's fun to point it out.

11. ST. JAMES' & GREEN PARK

These parks make up some of the prettiest green spaces in London. Saint James Park is famous for its pelicans, flamingos, deer, squirrels, black swans, ducks, and other water birds. Green Park has beautiful old trees and fun open-air stalls selling crafts and souvenirs.

Saint James' Park. *Between Buckingham Palace and Whitehall, south of The Mall and north of Birdcage Walk. Tube: Saint James Park*

This is one of London's loveliest spots. Your kids may recognize it from the film *101 Dalmatians* (the version with real people, not the animated one). It's where both the human and Dalmatian dog couples first meet. Saint James Park is a wonderful place to come relax after a visit to Buckingham Palace or through the Cabinet War Rooms. You can sit on the grass, have a snack, and watch the frolicking squirrels and birds. The pelican are fed each day at 3, and are said to descend from a pair offered to King Charles II by the Russian Ambassador in 1662. From the bridge in the middle of the lake, there are wonderful views (and photo opportunities!) of Buckingham Palace on one side and Whitehall on the other.

Before it was a park, Saint James was a swamp bordered by a leper colony. During the reign of Henry VIII the swamp was drained so that the king could raise and hunt deer there. In the 17th century, King Charles II decided to turn the area into a park. He hired the French landscape architect André LeNôtre (responsible for the gardens at Versailles) to do the design.

Saint James Palace. *Cleveland Row and Marlboro Road. Tube: Green Park. Note: The palace is not open to the public.*

This palace was built by King Henry VIII on the grounds of a former leper hospital. It has long been a favorite Royal Residence – used by Elizabeth I, James, I, Charles I, and Charles II. The current Princes Charles, William, and Harry have offices here, as does Princess Anne.

There are two sentries who guard the palace entrance, under the clock tower. They offer great photo opportunities, and you can watch the **changing of the guard** each day (every other day in the winter) around 11:30.

Green Park. *Along Piccadilly, between St. James' Park and Hyde Park. Tube: Green Park, Hyde Park Corner.*

This is the smallest of London's Royal Parks. The name reflects the fact that this park contains vast lawns and large trees, but no colorful flowerbeds. It was laid out during the reign of King Henry VIII in an area that served as a burial ground for the Saint James Leper Hospital nearby. The park also follows a line formed by the former Tyburn River.

During the 18th century, Green Park was a popular spot for duels, balloon rides, and fireworks. George Frederick Handel wrote his Royal Fireworks music in honor of a celebration for the Peace of Aix-la-Chapelle that took place here in 1748.

When the weather is nice you can walk along the Piccadilly edge of Green Park and check out the wide variety of stands that sell books, jewelry, crafts, and other fun items.

Saint James' Church. *197 Piccadilly, W1. Tube: St. James Park or Westminster.*

This church was designed by Sir Christopher Wren, and it was one of his favorite accomplishments. There is an **arts and crafts market** in the courtyard every Wed-Sat, and an **antiques market** on Tues. There are also regular lunchtime and evening **concerts**.

12. HYDE PARK, KENSINGTON, & KNIGHTSBRIDGE

Although these neighborhoods are pretty posh, they also contain some of the most family-friendly sights in London. You'll get a taste of royalty in Kensington Palace, fantasy in the Peter Pan-inspired playground, and luxury at Harrod's Department Store. This is also where you'll find great green spaces and some of London's best kid-oriented museums.

Hyde Park, London. W2. Tube: Lancaster Gate, Marble Arch, Hyde Park Corner, and Knightsbridge. Open daily, 5am-midnight.

Hyde Park, one of the largest public parks in London, was once a royal hunting ground purchased by King Henry VIII from the monks of Westminster. King James I first opened the park to non-royals, although access was still limited to fashionable people. By the reign of Charles I, Hyde Park was open to the general public. When the Great Plague struck London in 1665, many Londoners camped out in Hyde Park to try to escape the unhealthy streets and houses of the city. By the late 17th century, however, Hyde Park had developed a nasty reputation – having become the site of muggings, hangings, and duels. Eventually the park regained its luster and became a location for great national events: a huge fireworks display to celebrate the end of the Napoleonic Wars in 1814, the Great Exhibition in 1851, and festivities in honor of Queen Elizabeth's Silver and Golden Jubilees.

Today, Hyde Park offers a bucolic break from the hustle and bustle of the city. There is a Lookout Center where children can learn about nature. There are 100-year-old trees and

enormous pigeons. There are rowboat and paddleboat rentals on the **Serpentine Lake**. Informal sports are played on the **sports fields** between Rotten Row and South Carriage Drive. Lounge chairs dot the greens between April and September (there's a small rental fee). There are **bike** and **skateboarding** paths in the park, as well as paths used for **walking** and **jogging**. There are facilities for **playing tennis, lawn bowling, horseback riding**, and **swimming** (see below).

On the west side of the Serpentine Lake is the **Princess Diana Memorial Fountain** – a tribute to her and her love of children.

The **Speakers' Corner** is on the NE tip of the park. Since 1872, this has the place where members of the public are allowed to come speak their minds openly on Sunday afternoons. Although many of the speakers are there to share pretty kooky views on religion or politics, the tradition of the Speakers' Corner provides a good opportunity to remind children that not everyone in the world gets to live in a country where they can openly voice their views in public.

On the northern side of the park, in the middle of a busy traffic island, you can see **Marble Arch**. Officially, only members of the Royal Family and important guests are allowed to walk through the middle of Marble Arch, but considering its location, who would want to? It marks the place formerly known as Tyburn Gallows - London's main public execution spot until 1783. Marble Arch originally stood in the courtyard entrance of Buckingham Palace. It was moved here in 1851, because it was too narrow for the Royal State Coach to pass through. The Arch contains three little rooms that were used as a police station until 1950. During the Hyde Park Riots of 1855, police officers hid inside the Arch and caught several of the riots' ringleaders by surprise.

On the SE corner of Hyde Park is a new **memorial**, erected to honor the 52 people killed by terrorist bombings in London on 7 July 2005.

On the SE edge of Hyde Park you can see **Wellington Arch** (technically called Constitution Arch). Built in 1828, it celebrates the British victories over Napoleon. The arch was originally located at the nearby Apsley House and was topped with a statue of the Duke of Wellington, who defeated Napoleon at Waterloo. Since 1912, the top of Wellington Arch has featured a bronze statue that shows Peace descending from Heaven onto the Quadriga (harness of four horses) of War. While the sculpture was being completed, eight workers had a dinner on top of one of the horses. Inside Wellington Arch there are three floors of exhibits on its history. From the arch's balcony, there are good views of Buckingham Palace and the Houses of Parliament.

Each morning the **Queen's Cavalry Guard** ride from their barracks in Hyde Park over to Horse Guards Row for the Whitehall Changing of the Guard. Watch for them around 10:30.

Kensington Gardens. *W8. Tube: Queensway or Notting Hill Gate.*

These gardens were originally part of Hyde Park. In 1728, Queen Caroline ordered the transformation of the gardens and oversaw the creation of the Serpentine and Long Water. They were closed to the public until the late 18th century, and even then were only open to people who were respectably dressed.

Today, Kensington Gardens are formal and well manicured, although the people strolling through don't have to dress up anymore. The gardens are a favorite spot for **strollers, joggers**, and **kite-flyers**. Deckchairs are available (small fee) for sunbathers in warm months. **Birdwatchers** keep track of the 170 or more bird species that visit or live in the gardens, including rare Green Woodpeckers. There are **bicycle** and **roller blading** paths.

Current and future sailing aficionados will enjoy watching the **model sail boats** on the Round Pond. The London Model Yacht Sailing Association and Model Yacht Club sponsor races on Sundays from 10 to 1. The boats really look like miniatures of world-class racers, and the rules are as formal as those of full-size yacht races.

On the southern side of the park, there is an extravagant **Memorial to Prince Albert**, the beloved husband of Queen Victoria who died of typhoid in 1861. She mourned his death and wore black for the rest of her life. The memorial depicts the prince clutching a catalogue from the Great Exhibition of 1851, which he helped plan. There are also statues representing the continents of America, Asia, Europe, and Africa.

Children will be more interested in hunting for the statue of **Peter Pan**, closer to the N side of the park by the Long Water. Those who know the story well will remember that it is here in Kensington Gardens that Peter runs away to live with the fairies and never grow up. The book's author, J.M. Barrie, lived near Kensington Gardens in the early 1900s and liked to walk here each day.

There is also an interesting statue nearby on Lancaster Walk devoted to physical energy. Another sculpture that's a hit with kids is known as the **Elfin Oak**. This is a hollowed tree stump, which has been carved with figures of little fairies, elves, and animals. It stands in the NW section of the park by the entrance to the Princess Diana playground.

Princess Diana Memorial Playground. *Near Black Lion Gate, Broad Walk, in Kensington Gardens, NW side. Tube: Bayswater or Queensway. Open daily, 10-dusk. Admission is free, but adults are only admitted if they are accompanied by children.*

Princess Diana lived in Kensington Palace and liked to come to the gardens for a stroll or jog. She was also a former kindergarten teacher and loved children. This playground was built in her memory. It is actually built on the same sight that once held a playground funded by J.M. Barrie, author of *Peter Pan*. The Princess Diana playground is filled with features from the Peter Pan stories. There's a big pirate ship with rigging, crow's nests, and secret passages between the decks. Around it is a sandy beach with sculpted crocodiles. There's a tree-house camp, equipped with tree-phones. Kids can look for Tiger Lily in the Indian teepees, sit on lamb-shaped benches, or make splashes in the mermaid's fountain. Even the public restrooms are called the Home Under Ground for the Lost Boys, and the windows are etched with illustrations from Peter Pan. Extras include a musical garden and a Victorian drinking fountain. It is a beautifully maintained playground, and much of it is accessible to children with special needs.

Kensington Palace. *Kensington Gardens, W8. Tube: Queensway, High Street Kensington, or Notting Hill Gate. Open 10-6 (Mar-Oct), 10-5 (Nov-Feb). Adults £12.50, Kids 5-16 £6.25, Kids under 5: free, Family (up to 2 adults/3kids): £34. Tickets are slightly less expensive if you book them online.*

Kensington Palace is most well known as having been the favorite residence of Diana, Princess of Wales.

The visit to this palace is undergoing reconstruction and will re-open as the Enchanted Palace, focused on the seven princesses, including Diana, who have lived there.

Serpentine Gallery. *Near Albert Memorial, Kensington Gardens, W2, Tube: South Kensington or Lancaster Gate. Open daily, 10-6. Admission: free.*

This building is a study in contrasts. On the outside it's a 1930's era teahouse and looks perfectly proper. Inside, however, it is filled with dramatic, contemporary art exhibits. In the past, exhibits have included greats such as Man Ray, Andy Warhol, and Henry Moore. Current exhibits can be interesting but also controversial, so look carefully at the exhibit posters, and don't be afraid to ask at the entrance if it is suitable for kids. Having said this, the Serpentine tries to be kid-friendly and sponsors workshops and educational activities for children. Since admission is free, it's easy to come and go. It's also interesting to note that sometimes children can surprise you by seeing sense in contemporary art that escapes adult perceptions.

South of Kensington Gardens, below the Albert Memorial are a number of important buildings. The **Royal College of Art** is a surprisingly unadorned brick building where many great artists, architects, designers, and other craftsmen have been formed. Next door is the building of the **Royal College of Organists**, decorated with friezes featuring musical instruments. The imposing round building is the **Royal Albert Hall**, which holds all sorts of musical, political, and sports events, including the summer Proms concerts.

Across Prince Consort Road there are other illustrious institutions: the **Royal School of Mines, Imperial College of Science and Technology**, and **Royal College of Music**, which has an interesting Museum of Instruments. (Note: Its hours are irregular, so call ahead: 020 7591 4346 or choose instead to visit the fine musical instrument collection at the nearby Victoria and Albert Museum). The 280 foot **Queen's Tower** on Imperial College Road dates from the late 1800s. It is across from a building dedicated to **Alexander Fleming**, the father of penicillin.

Beyond these are three museums that are a big hit with visitors young and old: the Science Museum, Museum of Natural History, and the Victoria and Albert Museum.

Victoria and Albert Museum. *Cromwell Road, South Kensington, SW7: Tube: South Kensington. Open daily 10-5:45 (10-10 on Wed). Admission is free, although there may be a charge for special exhibits.*

Note: This is an incredibly **kid-friendly museum** and much more of a hit with all members of the family than you might expect! There are three hands-on **Discovery Areas** full of fun activities ranging from dressing up as Sherlock Holmes to designing your own family crest. The galleries have "**Please Touch**" activities and **headphones** for listening to music of different eras. You can borrow an **Activity Backpack** filled with puzzles, games, and props related to the British Galleries (and to a series of other

themes during school holidays). **An Activity Cart** roams through the museum on Sundays and during school vacations with hands-on activities for kids ages 3-12. There are also **Family Trails** on different topics that you can pick up at the Information Desks and enjoy together. **Family events and young peoples' programs** are offered during school vacations ranging from drawing and creative sessions to storytelling, performance arts, and digital photography. And for teens and adults, there are **activity packs on drawing and creative writing** available on loan at the Grand Entrance.

This museum was designed following the Great Exhibition of 1851 to make works of art accessible to everyone. It also became a showcase for some of the greatest examples of art and design from Europe and former British colonies. All this might sound quite boring, but it's not, because the museum is so user-friendly and interactive.

Avid clothes shoppers will enjoy looking through the museum's fashion section that offers examples of clothing designs from around the world and across the ages. Budding musicians can check out a wide collection of musical instruments – some of which are displayed in large cases that you have to pull out and push back in. Fans of chivalry will get a kick out of trying on a real armored gauntlet in the Tudor section. That's where you can also admire one of the world's largest beds, known as the Great Bed of Ware. It is 9 feet wide, 10 feet high, and big enough to sleep eight people. You can also look at some of the world's smallest portraits in this section, including a miniature of Anne of Cleves, who was one of Henry VIII's six wives. He decided that she looked better in miniature than in real life and quickly divorced her.

The Victorian section has lots of elaborate furniture and decorative arts. There's a charming black and white dog made of porcelain and a Chippendale bed made to look like a Chinese temple. You can build your own Crystal Palace in the discovery area or try on a hoop skirt. In the 18th century part, you can see some well-dressed male and female dolls, and admire extra outfits for them displayed in pull-out drawers beneath the exhibit case. One of the most memorable pieces in the Asian collection is

Tipu's Tiger. This is an odd wooden carving that portrays a tiger biting the throat of a British Officer. A miniature organ inside the sculpture plays the sounds of the tiger's roars and man's cries. It was designed for a Sultan named Tipu, in the 1790s.

Throughout the museum there are lots of things to open, touch, and explore as well as interactive computer stations.

Natural History Museum. *Cromwell Road SW7. Tube: South Kensington. Open Mon-Sat 10-5; Sun 2-5. Admission is Free.*

Note: Kids love Natural History museums anyway, but this one also has many hands-on exhibits, gallery trails and activity sheets (50 pence), and free loan of pencils, paper, and clipboards

This place is cool even before you walk in the main entrance. On the outside is a garden with animal statues, and the front of the building is covered with decorative sculptures of plants and animals. Just a few examples of the things you'll see and do inside are seeing a model of a blue whale, feeling the earth shake beneath your feet, admiring rare gems, visiting prehistoric animals, or watching leafcutter ants, or looking at all sorts of animals big and small.

Science Museum. *Exhibition Road, SW7 (next to the Natural History Museum) Tube: South Kensington. Open daily: 10-6. Free admission, though there is a charge for special exhibits and IMAX movies.*

Note: **Children's Trail Guides** on space travel, materials, cuts and cures, flight, and "Medicine's Murky Past" are sold at the bookshop and sales desks. You can also rent a an **audioguide** for £3.50 that tells funny and factual stories about the Space, Making Power, and Modern World Galleries on the museum's ground floor.

This is a fun, hands-on museum that explores science in many forms and across many ages. You can go from medieval medicine to space travel, or from the science of sports to computer technologies. There are exhibits on engines, materials, weather, agriculture, how to measure time, make paper, go diving, or pass into virtual reality.

The museum is highly interactive, with zones tailored for kids of different ages. Little kids can play with light, sound, and water. They can beam a whisper across a gallery or build a bridge to walk across. Older kids can explore the makings of objects from everyday life, take the controls of a cockpit, or go on the air with a working radio station. In Digitopolis, kids can explore the ways digital and virtual technologies are changing our world. There's a whole section on the history of medicine, from prehistoric times to the present, including veterinary medicine, too.

Baden-Powell House. *Hostel and Scouting Museum. 65-67 Queens Gate, SW7. Tel 020 7584 7031. Tube: Gloucester Road or South Kensington. Open daily. Museum is free.*

This building was erected to honor Lord Robert Baden-Powell, the founder of international scouting. Today, the Baden-Powell house contains accommodations for families, groups, and individuals. There are also conference rooms and a small museum, which traces the history of scouting.

Kensington Village. **Kensington High Street** is filled with bookstores, boutiques, and shops. If you are looking for hip girls' clothes you can try **Miss Selfridge** at #42-44. The small but well-stocked **Children's Book Centre** at #237 has books arranged by age groupings as well as selections of toys and videos.

Further down, the glass, tent-shaped building with a copper roof is the **Commonwealth Institute**. Opened in 1962 it features exhibit galleries and performance spaces for dance, music, and theatrical productions from all 50 of the British Commonwealth countries. Behind this building is a large sports field and green space called **Holland Park**. In the middle stands **Holland House**, which was once a favorite meeting spot for authors such as Charles Dickens, Wordsworth, and Lord Byron. The East Wing of this 16th century mansion serves as a Youth Hostel. The front courtyard of Holland House serves as an open-air theater in the summer months, featuring mainly opera and dance performances. There is a pretty Japanese Garden in the Park where you can watch peacocks as they strut their stuff and display their magnificent plumes.

Knightsbridge. *East of Kensington and South of Hyde Park. Tube: Knightsbridge.*

This is a very ritzy part of town, best known for its high-end shopping.

Harvey Nichols Department Store. *Corner of Knightsbridge and Sloane Street. SW1. Open 10-7 Mon-Tues; 10-8 Wed-Fri; 10-7 Sat; 12-6 Sun.*

This was reputedly one of Princess Diana's favorite stores. The gourmet foods are on the fifth floor. Even if you don't go in, take a look at the fanciful window displays.

Harrod's Department Store. *87-135 Brompton Road. SW1. Tube: Knightsbridge. Open Mon-Sat, 10-7.*

Harrod's is worth a visit even if you don't buy a thing. Originally started as a small tea and soap shop run by Henry Harrod and two employees, it has become the *nec plus ultra* in upscale shopping. Be warned however that you will be expected to look the part – no torn jeans or

backwards baseball caps allowed. You can have fun just admiring the fancy fashions or enjoying the beauty of the building. At night the whole place lights up like a Christmas tree. Inside there are some palace-like rooms with marble and chandeliers, big stuffed leather chairs (even in the men's room I'm told), or remarkable Egyptian motifs. Don't miss the **food hall** on the ground level. It's filled with impressive displays, imaginative decorations, and endless varieties of gourmet foods (*see photo below*). The second floor has a pampered pet section (*see photo above*). Kids' toys and games are on the 4th floor. On the lower level by the Egyptian escalator, there is a memorial to Princess Diana and Dodi Al Fayed (whose father owns Harrods).

13. CHELSEA & BATTERSEA PARK

The history of Chelsea is as colorful and ever-changing as many of the fashions that adorn its shops and boutiques. Once the domain of kings, Chelsea has been home to bohemian writers, rock stars, and the original English punks. It was the birthplace of Dracula – at least the fictional one. The real Count Dracula was from Transylvania, but the novel about him was written in Chelsea by author Bram Stoker in 1897. Today, the neighborhood features a famous flower show, a botanical garden, and home for disabled war veterans, along with its shops and restaurants.

For kids, there are lots of fun distractions across the river in Battersea Park where they can find a children's zoo, goofy bicycles, boating lakes, and lots of other activities.

Kings Road. *Chelsea. SW3. Tube: Sloane Square.*

In the 18th and early 19th centuries, this road was closed off to anyone but those holding a special Royal Pass. It was also the path used by King Charles II to visit his mistress Nell Gwynne who lived on Fulham Road.

Today, King's Road is lined with clothing and shoe shops, nice restaurants, a movie theater, the Chelsea Young People's Theater, and children's stores.

At the eastern end of Kings Road is **Sloane Square**. There is a famous department store here specialized in home furnishings, called Peter Jones. Opposite this store is a new pedestrian district named after the Duke of York.

Chelsea Physic Garden. *66 Royal Hospital Road, SW3. Tube Sloane Square. Open Apr-Nov, Wed 12-5, Sun 2-6. Adults £8; Kids 5-15 and Students £5; Under 5 free.*

This garden (*photo at left*) was founded in 1673 by the Society of Apothecaries. Its main purpose was to grow medicinal plants and test new plant species. Hans Sloane, who was King George II's personal physician, insisted that the gardens experiment with 50 new plant species each year. Most were imported from far-away lands, including the cottonseed that would eventually launch the cotton industry in the American South. Today, the Garden contains some 7,000 different kinds of plants and many are still used for research and education.

Each year the **Chelsea Flower Show** is held in May on the grounds of the Royal Hospital. It is a world-famous event and quite extravagant. The first two days are reserved for members of the Royal Horticultural Society, but on the final day, the display plants are sold off to the general public.

Chelsea Football Club Stadium Tours. *Stamford Bridge, Fulham Road, SW6. Tube: Fulham Broadway. Tours of the stadium take place daily every half hour 11-3, if there is no match taking place. Regular Tour – Adults £15, Kids £9.*

Soccer fans take note! Chelsea Football Club is the largest professional soccer club in London and the team has enjoyed many wins. The stadium tours take you behind the scenes, into the locker rooms, dugout, press room, through the players' tunnel, onto the pitch, and up to the best seats in the stadium. You can learn about players' pre-game rituals, see their seats and jerseys, and learn about how the security and technology work in the stadium. Don't forget your camera!

Regular tours last 1.5 hours. There is also a special tour where your host will be Stamford the Lion, the official Chelsea team mascot. He delights kids and gives everyone a special souvenir at the end of the visit.

Battersea Park. *SW 11. South Bank of the Thames, between Albert Bridge and Chelsea Bridge. Tube: Sloane Square. Open sunrise to sunset.*

This park is a former dueling ground that was converted to a beautiful green space during the Victorian Era (*see photo on next page*). It has woods, lawns, and plenty of wildlife. Features include a lake for boating, a children's zoo, a field with deer, many wild birds, and a Japanese Peace Pagoda. There are tennis courts, soccer fields, adventure playgrounds, and lots of open spaces to run around. There is also a spot that rents funny bicycles.

There are tons of special events at Battersea Park. There's a special Teddy Bear Picnic on the first Friday in August and open air concerts in summer. Other events include a zoo Easter Egg Hunt, Easter Parade, Horse Parade, World Parrot Day, Police Dog Show, Fireworks, May Day Parade, and many others.

Battersea Park Children's Zoo. *Open daily 10-5 (Apr-Sep); only on weekends 11-3 (Oct-Mar). Adults £2; Kids 2-15 £1; Kids under 2 free.*

This cute little zoo has small, kid-sized animals like pot-bellied pigs, marmosets, meerkats, miniature Shetland ponies, goats, and more.

Bike Rentals – London Recumbents (near the tennis courts in Battersea Park). *Open weekends and holidays 10-dark. Rentals range from £7-£15 per hour depending on the bike.*

This place rents all sorts of fun adult and kid-sized bicycles, starting with recumbents but also including banana bikes, side-by-sides, Giant EZ bikes, and more.

14. BRITISH MUSEUM, BLOOMSBURY, & HOLBORN

Bloomsbury is the intellectual heart of London, home to the University of London, London School of Economics, and Virginia Woolf's circle of literary friends known as the "Bloomsbury Group". Kids will be more impressed by the treasure-hunting adventures offered at the British Museum, great playground facilities of Coram's Fields, and visible relics of the stories of Charles Dickens. There's also a tribute to a literary figure they can really appreciate – Harry Potter.

British Museum. *Great Russell Street, London WC1. Open Sat-Wed, 10-5:30 and Thurs-Fri, 10–8:30. Tube: Holborn. Entrance is Free. Audio tour headsets are £3.50. There is a separate audio tour for the Elgin Marbles from the Parthenon. Guided tours (1.5 hours) are available-Prices vary.*

Note: This museum is full of family-friendly activities. There are free **family trails**, and free **Activity Backpacks** full of puzzles, games, and activities associated with the exhibits. You can borrow crayons and pads for free, or rent the **Children's Multimedia Guide** for £3.

The sheer size of this museum will strike you when you first walk in and see the glass-covered Great Court. The British Museum welcomes more than 5.4 million visitors a year and contains some of the world's greatest treasures, such as the Rosetta Stone (which helped unlock the secrets of Egyptian hieroglyphics) and the Elgin Marbles (*photo at right*), which originally decorated the façade of the Parthenon in Athens. There are Greek and Roman masterpieces, Egyptian mummies, Anglo-Saxon trea-

sures, Assyrian palace sculptures, Mexican artifacts, and artistic wonders from Asia, the Near East, and India. European art and artifacts span the range from the Bronze Age to the 20th century. There's even an exhibit on the evolution of money. Altogether there are more than 7 million objects housed at the British Museum, within 2 1/2 miles of galleries.

All this would be terribly overwhelming if it weren't for the fact that the museum goes to great lengths to make itself family-friendly. Besides, since the entrance is free, you don't have to feel compelled to see it all at once. Just pick out your top choices, and leave the rest for another day.

Here's a brief review of some of the Museum's highlights:

Ancient Assyria and Mesopotamia: Winged bulls from Palace of Sargon II (notice how they have five legs and look on the base to see where bored palace guards hand etched a game board). Cuneiform tablets (that show the earliest form of writing); other sculptures and reliefs from palaces of Nimrud, Nineveh, and Khorsabad; Flood Tablet telling the Epic of Gilgamesh.

Ancient Persia: Gold, silver, and bronze treasures.

Ancient Egypt: Rosetta Stone (written in Greek and hieroglyphics, it offered key to deciphering hieroglyphs); mummies; colossal bust of Ramses II and other statues, including interesting animal gods.

Ancient Greece and Rome: Elgin Marbles (statues depicting processions for the Festival of Athena from the triangular pediments of the Parthenon on the Acropolis); statues, vases, burial art.

Americas : Treasures of the Olmec and Maya; Native American masks, totems, clothing, jewelry; Easter Island statues.

Britain: Lindow Man (Iron Age fellow found in peat bog); Gold body-chain from the Hoxne hoard (Roman Era); Neptune Dish of Mildenhall (Roman Era); Treasures from ship-burial at Sutton Hoo (Anglo-Saxon); Viking treasures; Lewis Isle chessmen (12th c.); Sloane astrolabe (AD 1200);

Asia: Korean ceramics; Chinese Tomb figures; jade; Lacquerware; paintings.

Africa: Yoruba, Kuba, and Kongo carvings and masks.

Library of the British Museum. *Reading Room, British Museum.*

This is a branch of the British Library, similar to the U.S. Library of Congress, where copies of every item printed in the United Kingdom are kept. Founded in 1753, the British Library has many important original manuscripts, such as the Magna Carta, Leonardo da Vinci's notebook, Alice in Wonderland, Jane Austin novels, Beatles' lyrics, and old fairy tales.

Platform 9 3/4. *Kings Cross Railway Station. NW1. Tube: Kings Cross*
This is a photo opportunity that no true Harry Potter fan will want to miss! You will have to look for a bit to find platform 9 3/4, but after all it's not supposed to be visible to non-magic folks. (Hint: follow platform 8 for a while, then turn left). You may not get to see the Hogwarts Express, but you'll see plenty of other interesting trains bound for destinations such as Cambridge and cities in Scotland.

Cartoon Museum. *35 Little Russell Street. WC1._Tube: Tottenham Court Road or Holborn. Open Tues-Sat, 10:30-5:30; Sun, 12-5:30. Adults: £5.50, Kids under 18: free.*

This museum has thousands of British cartoons, caricatures, and comics from the 18th century to the present. There are family fun days with cartoon classes every second Saturday of the month and other activities for kids.

London Canal Museum. *12-13 New Wharf Road, N1. Open Tues-Sun, 10-4:30. Closed Mon and Sat. Adults £3, Kids 8-15 £1.50, Kids under 5 are free. Tube: Kings Cross. Special summer activities for kids are offered daily in August at 11 and 1:30 for a fee of £4 per children (free for accompanying adults).*

Note: You can download an audio tour on your MP3 player from www.canalmuseum.org.uk.

This museum tells the story of London's canals. You can learn all about the people and horses that worked with canal boats and the cargo they carried. Visitors can go inside a canal boat cabin, look at model boats, and learn to tie knots. You can also view an underground icehouse that was located beneath the museum's building and was used to store ice imported on boats from Norway in the days before refrigeration. The icehouse was built for a Swiss-Italian entrepreneur who sold ice and ice cream.

Coram's Fields Children's Playground. *93 Guildford Street, WC1, Tube: Russell Square. Open Mon-Sat, 9-8 (or dusk); Sun, 12-5.*

This 7-acre playground is only open to adults who come accompanied by a child. It occupies the site of a former orphanage. There are lots of things to climb on and swing from, a basketball court, sports fields, a sandpit, toddler's gym, and more. Summer activities may include entertainers or arts and crafts.

Sir John Soane Museum. *13, Lincoln's Inn Fields (N. side of the Square) WC2. Tube: Holborn. Open Tues-Sat 10-5. Closed Mon. Every first Tues of the month there is an evening candlelit visit from 6-9. Admission is free. Special audiotours are available for kids and adults, and can be downloaded to your MP3 player from www.soaneeducation.org.uk/children/audio_tours.cfm.*

Note: there are special full or half-day workshops for kids during school vacations.

Walking through this museum feels like an odd combination of your eccentric great-grandmother's attic and a movie set for *Indiana Jones*. It is comprised of a series of town houses owned by Sir John Soane (1753-1837), who is considered to be one of England's most important architects. Soane designed and lived in the buildings that contain his museum, filling them with interesting domes, archways, and lighting effects. The rooms alone are worth the visit, but Soane was also an avid collector of art, archeological artifacts, and architectural documents. These are displayed as he kept them, according to no particular order or theme. The result is a fantastic mish-mash of treasures, including paintings by Hogarth, Turner, and Canaletto; busts, urns, pieces of architectural details, an Egyptian sarcophagus, and much much more.

Old Curiosity Shop. *13 Portsmouth Street. WC2. By the SW corner of Lincoln's Inn Fields. Tube: Holborn*

Fans of Charles Dickens will enjoy seeing (and photographing) the façade of this tiny shop, named for one of his novels.

Dickens' House Museum. *48 Doughty Street, London, WC1. Tube: Russell Square. Open daily, 10-5 (until 7 on Tues). Adults: £6, Kids £3, Family (2 adult + up to 3 kids £15.*

Charles Dickens lived in 22 different houses throughout London, but this is the only one that remains today. It is here that he wrote his great classics *Oliver Twist, Pickwick Papers*, and *Nicholas Nickleby*. The Dickens' House Museum displays portraits, letters, and books from Dickens' daily life. There is also a recreation of the Dingley Dell Kitchen portrayed in *Pickwick Papers*. If you visit during the Christmas holidays, the house will be decorated as it would have been in Dickens' day and you can try out hot mince pies or mulled wine.

Just for background: When he was a boy, Charles Dickens' family became destitute. He had to leave school and work in a rat-infested factory. This is why stories of poverty and the hard-hearted response of Victorian upper-class society appear so frequently in his books. As an adult he fought

for the reform of English poor laws and abolition of the slave trade. Each year a wreath is placed on his memorial in Westminster Abbey as a tribute to his work, both as a writer and as a reformer.

15. REGENT'S PARK, BAKER STREET, & ABBEY ROAD

This part of town really has something for everyone. There are playgrounds and a magnificent zoo for little kids. There's blood and gore at Madame Tussaud's Wax Museum. Amateur sleuths can look for clues in the Sherlock Holmes Museum. Kids with a dramatic flair can enjoy the frolics of a Midsummer Night's Dream at the Open-Air Theatre. And finally, Beatles fans can follow the footsteps of the fabulous four to Abbey Lane and Primrose Hill.

Regent's Park. *NW1, Tube: Regent's Park or Baker Street. Open daily, dawn-dusk.*

In the days of King Henry VIII this area was part of the royal hunting grounds. Today it features such elements as a splendid rose garden, called **Queen Mary's Garden**, a lake filled with graceful water birds, and a Japanese bridge. In the summer the pristine lawns are covered in deck chairs, available for lounging (for a small fee).

More active visitors will find playing fields, tennis courts, a running track and plenty of paths for jogging, three children's playgrounds, and even a baseball diamond. You can rent a canoe or sailboat on the **large lake**. Kids can rent their own paddleboats that they can maneuver through the shallow waters of the **Children's Lake**. When it's time for a break, there's a nice café. If you want cultural entertainment there's a music gazebo that holds summer concerts and an open-air theater.

Open-Air Theater. *Inner Circle, Queen Mary's Gar-*

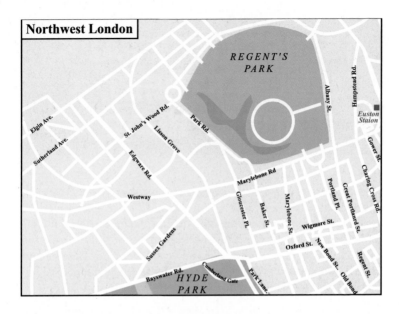

Northwest London

REGENT'S PARK

HYDE PARK

Elgin Ave.

Sutherland Ave.

St. John's Wood Rd.

Lisson Grove

Park Rd.

Albany St.

Hampstead Rd.

Euston Staion

Gower St.

Edgware Rd.

Westway

Marylebone Rd

Charing Cross Rd.

Great Portland St.

Portland Pl.

Gloucester Pl.

Baker St.

Marylebone St.

Wigmore St.

Oxford St.

New Bond St.

Regent St.

Old Bond

Sussex Gardens

Bayswater Rd.

Cumberland Gate

Park Lane

den, *Regent's Park, NW1, Tube: Baker Street. Matinee and evening perfor-mances, Jun-Sep, weather permitting. Online information at www.openairtheatre.org/ Phone information: 020 7486 2431.*

This theater is in a lovely setting surrounded by roses. It offers quality classical productions, with plenty of Shakespeare. *A Midsummer Night's Dream* is generally on the play list at some point during the summer. Some shows are specially designed for kids, such as *Wind in the Willows*, which was playing when we were there. People line up early for tickets, so you may want to reserve them ahead of time on-line or by phone. If it rains, you won't be reimbursed but you will be issued new tickets for another date.

London Zoo. *Outer Circle, NE corner of Regent's Park, NW1, Tube: Camden Town or Baker Street (transfer to the 274 bus to avoid a long walk). Open daily 10-5:30 (Mar-Oct), 10-4 (Nov-Feb). Adults £18; Kids 3-15 £14; Kids under 3 free; Family ticket (2 adults/2kids or 1 adult/3 kids) £58.*

Note: If you have the time, a fun way to go to the zoo is **by canal boat**, cruising down the Regent's Canal from Little Venice (Blomfield Road, W9, Warwick Ave. Tube) or Camden Lock (Chalk Farm Rd, NW1, Camden Town Tube). The **London Waterbus Company** runs a regular service from 10 to 5 each day from Apr to Sep and on weekends Oct-Mar. One-way fares (including entrance to the Zoo) from Little Venice or Camden Lock are Adult: £19.50, Child: £16.50. Round-trip fares are an additional £4 for adults or £3 for kids.

The London Zoo was originally a scientific study center where only Fellows of the Zoological Society were admitted. The animals were donated by scientists, diplomats, sailors, and collectors from all over the world. Some had belonged to the Royal Family. Most of the animals arrived by ship. Larger ones often finished the journey on foot, walking several miles from the docks along the Thames to the zoo. The zoo's first giraffes went into a panic as they crossed the city and ran into a cow in Commercial Road. Tommy, the zoo's first chimpanzee, arrived in style aboard a stagecoach in 1835.

The London Zoological Park was opened to the public in 1847. It was the first to open a Reptile House in 1849, followed by the first public Aquarium (1853), the first Insect House (1881), and the first Children's Zoo (1938) inaugurated by young brothers, Robert and Ted Kennedy.

Another first was the adoption of the term *zoo*. Previously, one referred to a zoological park or garden. But in 1867 a popular London music hall singer called The Great Vance, sang a tune about "the OK thing to do on Sunday afternoon, is to toddle in the Zoo", and the new term caught on.

In the 1920s, two of the zoo's regular visitors were A.A. Milne and his young son, Christopher Robin. In fact, Winnie the Pooh is named for a black bear that lived at the zoo from 1914 to 1934. The zoo also inspired Milne to write these lines:

"There are lions and roaring tigers, and enormous camels and things;
There are biffalo-buffalo-bisons, and a great big bear with wings;
There's a sort of tiny potamus, and a tiny nosserus too –
But *I* gave buns to the elephant when *I* went down to the Zoo!"
– *When We Were Very Young*, A. A. Milne, 1924

Today, the zoo discourages feeding buns to the elephants but offers plenty of other fun things to do. London Zoo covers 36 acres and includes three areas, linked together by tunnels and bridges. There are more than 5,000 animals – many of them on the endangered species list. The types of animals range from large mammals to tiny insects. There are reptiles, fish, invertebrates, birds, and mammals. Most are exhibited in settings made to look as natural as possible.

The **Children's Zoo and Pet Care Centre** is a big hit with kids who can get up close to see alpacas, kangaroo, sheep, goats, rabbits, chinchillas, budgies, and familiar farm animals. At 3 pm, you can watch them milk the cows. In the summer there are pony and camel rides. Other points of interest include the **Globe Sundial, Old Clock Tower**, and the **Winnie the Bear Cub Memorial**.

The zoo proposes special **kid-friendly activities** on weekends during the school year and every day during school holidays. These range from opportunities to touch a snake skin, watch a predatory bird hunt, see a bird-eating spider, learn about kangaroos, or meet a meerkat to undertaking animal-inspired arts and crafts activities with zoo volunteers.

Some of the London Zoo's more memorable residents have included:

•**Obaysch**, the zoo's first hippopotamus. Brought to the zoo in 1850, it was the first animal of its kind to have been seen in Europe since the time of the Romans.

•**Guy**, a small gorilla who arrived at the zoo on Guy Fawkes day in 1947. When sparrows would fly into his enclosure, he would pick them up gently, look at them closely, and then let them go. There is a statue in his honor near the zoo entrance.

•**Josephine**, a great Indian hornbill bird who lived to be 53 years old.

•**Goldie**, a golden eagle who escaped from the zoo in 1965 and delighted Londoners for 12 days as she took to the air above the city rooftops. Her sightings caused traffic jams as people stopped to watch. She was recaptured and returned to the zoo.

•**Eros**, a snowy owl (like Harry Potter's Hedwig) who was born in the wild, became lost in a storm at sea in 1950, and landed as an exhausted bundle on the deck of the HMS Eros off the Azores Islands. He was brought to the zoo where he lived until 1993, fathering 57 chicks along the way.

•**Belinda**, a beloved Mexican red-kneed bird-eating spider who appeared on TV as a guest and in advertisements for the zoo. She did much to help people overcome their fear of spiders, and died at the age of 22 in 1993.

Madame Tussaud's Wax Museum. *Marlyborne Road, NW1 (on the S side of Regents Park). Tube: Baker Street. Opening times vary during the year, but generally run from about 9:30-5:30. Adults £28; Kids £24; family of four £99. You can save time and money by purchasing tickets online ahead of time at www.madame-tussauds.com*

Note: Cameras are allowed in most sections of the museum, so you can really have fun setting up portraits with your favorite celebrities or gory scenes.

Madame Tussaud was French (1761-1850) and started her career of making wax figures with wealthy nobles in Paris. She eventually moved to England where she set up a permanent exihibit here. She used real clothes and props from her models, including the actual guillotine blade used to chop off the head of France's King Louis XVI.

Today, Madame Tussaud's Wax Museum contains hundreds of figures. There are many contemporary ones, including popular singers, movie stars, British royalty, politicians, and sports heroes. These sometimes change or get moved around, so you may or may not see your favorite Hollywood idol. The wax figures are organized by groups and themes. Some of the historical ones are depicted in context, such as the arrest of Mary, Queen of Scots; the burning of religious reformer Martin Luther; or Admiral Nelson's death in the Battle of Trafalgar. These scenes can be quite interactive – with sound, light, and even smells.

The Chamber of Horrors has some of the oldest pieces in the collection, such as the severed head of Queen Marie Antoinette that was modeled from the real thing. The Chamber Live is supposed to be even more scary than the Chamber of Horrors. The Spirit of London section takes you through the city's history. In the Diva exhibit you can grab the mike and have your own American Idol moment or you can listen to fashion tips and celebrity gossip in the Blush section.

Sherlock Holmes Museum. *239 Baker Street, NW1. Tube: Baker Street. Open daily 9:30-6. Adults £6; Kids under 16 £4.*

Note: If your kids are too young for Sherlock Holmes, you can rent the movie, *The Great Mouse Detective*, which is a nice cartoon take on the Holmes stories.

This small museum celebrates the fictional adventures of Sherlock Holmes and Doctor Watson, set at 221b Baker Street in the late 19th century. It's a charming way to combine the facts of Victorian life with the fiction of Sir Arthur Conan Doyle. The house has faithfully maintained its Victorian furnishings and carefully presents many of the everyday items and memorabilia from the Sherlock Holmes' stories. You'll see the great detective's study and bedroom, including his famous magnifying glass, chemistry set, pipe, armchair, violin, Persian slippers, and deerstalker. Dr. Watson's room on the second floor contains his diary, with notes from the famous case of the *Hound of the Baskervilles*. The third floor has arrangements of wax models depicting characters from the Sherlock Holmes adventures, including the evil Professor Moriarty. You can even visit the attic room where trunks and luggage are stored. There are guides in period costume to welcome you and answer questions.

Primrose Hill. *North of Regent's Park, across Prince Albert Road from the London Zoo. Tube: St. John's Wood or Camden Town*

This hill, once a hangout for robbers, is 260 feet high. It is the spot where Paul McCartney used to walk his dog Martha (inspiration for the Beatles' White Album song *Martha, My Dear*). Hike to the top and you'll have a great view of the city. It's a popular place for picnickers and kite-flyers. There's plenty of room for kids to run and a small playground near the zoo-side entrance.

Each year on **Guy Fawkes Day** (5 November) effigies of the man who tried to blow up Parliament are burned in big bonfires. This is traditionally followed by a fireworks show. The display on Primrose Hill is considered to be one of the best in the city.

Abbey Road. *NW8. Tube: Saint John's Wood. From the tube station, walk along Grove End Road to Abbey Road where you will see the famous zebra crossing.*

On August 8, 1969 the Beatles did a photo shoot for their new album at a crosswalk (known as a zebra crossing for its black and white pole markers telling cars to stop) near their recording studio, immortalizing the spot forever. Today, tourists come from all over the world to emulate the famous Abbey Road album cover (*see photo on next page*). Some dress up in white or black suits like John and Ringo. Others go barefoot like Paul. A few are said to take off all their clothes!

No matter what you are wearing, the Abbey Road crosswalk is a fun photo opportunity for Beatles' fans young and old. Just remember to watch for traffic as you take the picture. Also don't expect a perfect match. The lines at the crosswalk have changed over time to include a white zigzag.

Down the street at #3 Abbey Road are the EMI studios where the Beatles recorded nearly all their songs. Out front, there is a wall where fans scribble messages in honor of the Fabulous Four. The wall is repainted every few days so it is an ever-changing monument to their enduring popularity. Inside, the studios continue to work in full swing, recording music with greats such as the Rolling Stones and U2. George Lucas records movie music there as well.

16. PADDINGTON STATION, NOTTING HILL, & LITTLE VENICE

This section of London, north and west of Hyde Park and Kensington Gardens, is notable for its streets and squares lined with Victorian townhouses, numerous bed/breakfasts, and ethnic restaurants. Thanks to plentiful bus lines and tube stops that connect it to the city's major sights, it's a popular place to stay for visiting families.

Paddington Train Station. *Praed Street. W2. Tube: Paddington.*

If you arrive in London via Heathrow Airport, you may be introduced to Paddington Train Station by way of the Heathrow Express, a rapid and convenient train that links London's major international airport with the city. As you make your way from the arrival platform to the station exit, look for the bronze statue of **Paddington Bear**, the delightful children's book character. With his wide-brimmed hat, he's a welcome sight for bleary-eyed travelers, young and old.

The character Paddington Bear was based on a stuffed animal that author Michael Bond discovered all alone on a shelf in Selfridges Department Store. He bought the bear and offered it to his wife. It inspired him to write a story about a little bear from the deepest, darkest Peru, who's

found sitting on a suitcase in Paddington Station wearing a tag marked, "Please look after this bear. Thank You." Little did he know that a lonely stuffed toy would bring him such fame. You can also catch trains here for southwest and western England and southern

Wales. While you are looking for the arrival and departure information, make sure to note the station's beautiful iron-girder roof.

Notting Hill. *London W11. Tube: Notting Hill Gate.*

This neighborhood was made famous by the movie *Notting Hill* starring Hugh Grant and Julia Roberts. It is a charming area and most well-known for its colorful **Portobello Road Market** *(see photo on next page).* During the week, the market vendors mainly sell food. But on Saturday, it expands to include antiques, jewelry, clothes, souvenirs, arts/crafts, and collectibles.

Each year during the last weekend of August, there's a **Notting Hill Carnival**. The flavor is Caribbean, as the area celebrates its diverse racial make-up.

Little Venice. *Behind Paddington Train Station. W9 Maida Vale. Tube: Warwick Avenue.*

The Little Venice neighborhood is lined with stately 17th century houses, big trees, and plentiful shops and eateries. The comparison with Venice is a bit exaggerated, but there are two canals: the Regent's Canal and the Grand Union Canal. They form a junction in Little Venice, creating a wide pool that surrounds a piece of land known as Browning's Island, named for the 19th century poet, Robert Browning, who lived nearby. It is very scenic, and includes kid-friendly activities such as a puppet theater on a barge and canal boat rides to the zoo.

The Puppet Theatre Barge. *Opposite 35 Blomfield Road, Little Venice W9. Tube: Warwick Avenue. For information call the box office: 07 836 202 745 or visit the website at www.puppetbarge.com. Adults £10; kids £8.50. Open at this site Dec-Jun.*

If you are visiting this area between December and June this is a great place to enjoy some of London's high quality theater for children. The Puppet Theatre Barge contains a 50-seat theater where both marionette and hand puppet shows are produced for family audiences. From July through October the barge travels to other sites along the Thames, such as Henley-on-Thames, Marlow, Cliveden, and Richmond-on-Thames.

Canal Boat Cruises. Several boat companies offer tours along Regent's Canal from Little Venice, by Regent's Park and the London Zoo, to Camden Town. Kids love the boat ride, and it gives you an opportunity to see London from a completely new perspective. Round-trip tours last about 90 minutes and are offered on a daily basis during the summer holidays or weekend basis during the school year. You can also opt for one-way trips, including a stop at the London Zoo. Call ahead to check times and confirm fares.

- **London Waterbus Company**. *Blomfield Road, W9. Little Venice. Tube: Warwick Avenue. Tel. 020 7482 2660.* Hourly service on historic canal boats from Little Venice to the Zoo and Camden during the summer. Weekend service during the school year. Prices vary according to the length and destination.
- **Jason's Canal Boat Trip**. *Opposite 42 Blomfield Road, W9, Little Venice. Tube: Warwick Avenue. Phone: 020 7286 3428.* 3-4 trips per day Apr-Oct, plus weekend service during the school year. Historic canal narrowboats leave from Jason's Warf for 11/2 -hour round trips to Camden Lock Market and back.

17. EAST END

Markets & Museum of Childhood

This area, east of London's financial district, is off the beaten track compared to standard tourist and shopping venues. For generations it's been home to working class Londoners, as well as waves of Jewish and South Asian immigrants. However, if you have a spirit for adventure or simply prefer flea markets to high fashion, it's well worth a visit. As a bonus, there are two museums that celebrate the imaginative spirit of childhood.

Spitalfields Market. *Commercial Street, between Lamb and Brushfield Streets, London E1. Tube: Liverpool Station. Open Mon-Fri 11-3; Sun:10-5. Organic Market: Fri, Sun.*

This large covered market dates back to the late 17th century. Today it is filled with stalls that feature arts, crafts, toys, souvenirs, and interesting clothes and accessories. There are plenty of organic food vendors and lots of stands selling a variety of ethnic foods – even BBQ. It's a good place to shop and have lunch.

On the Tuesday before Lent there is a **Pancake Day Race** here that involves teams of four contestants tossing pancakes in their frying pans as they run. Why pancakes? It comes from the tradition of making pancakes on Fat Tuesday (known as Shrove Tuesday in Britain) to use up stocks of butter before the 40 days of fasting during Lent.

Petticoat Lane Market. *Middlesex Street and Wentworth Street, London E1. Tube: Liverpool Station or Algate East. Open: Mon-Fri: 10-2:30; Sun: 9-2.*

The name Petticoat Lane comes from the fact that this open-air market was started by French Protestant lacemakers fleeing persecution in their own country. They sold not only lace but also new and used clothing. You can still find old and used clothing here (*see photo on next page*).

Brick Lane Market. *London E1. Tube: Allen Gardens or Algate East. Open Sun sunrise-noon.*

This market) is located east of the Petticoat Lane and Spitalfields Markets, in an area that once housed London's brickfields. These were used after the Great London Fire to help rebuild the city. There were also beer breweries, which have since been turned into art studios and lofts. On Sunday mornings there are open-air stalls selling fruits, vegetables, meats, and second-hand goods. During the week, the shops along Brick Lane also sell leather goods, shoes, clothes, and jewelry. You can also find Jewish delis and what is reputed to be some of the best Bengali and Indian food in the city.

Each year in September the neighborhood's cultural diversity is celebrated during the **Brick Lane Festival**. There's plenty of food, street entertainment, music, performances, and special activities for kids.

V &A Museum of Childhood. *Cambridge Heath Road, London, E2. Tube: Bethnal Green Tube. Open Mon-Thur and Sat 10- 5:50, Sun 2:30- 5:50. Admission is free.*

As if this museum weren't kid-friendly enough, **special children's activities** are offered each day free of charge, including storytelling, dance, music, treasure hunts, movement, or arts and crafts.

Adults love this place as much as kids, and why not? Who can resist a museum filled with toys? The museum contains the toys and kids costume collections from the Victoria and Albert Museum. These include a huge collection of dolls and dollhouses, puppets, toy trains and cars, optical toys, toy soldiers and action figures from different eras, stuffed toys, kids' furniture, dress-up costumes, games, and more. Many of the exhibits feature hands-on components, such as winding up a train, riding a rocking horse, challenging your companions in a board game, or designing your own virtual toy on the computer. Temporary exhibits focus on topics such as childhoods in other lands, the history of particular kinds of toys, children's art, or children's literature.

Discover Museum. *1 Bridge Terrace, Stratford, London, E15. This is located further to the NE in East London. Tube: Stratford Station (Central Line) or Docklands Light Railway beyond Greenwich to Stratford Station. Open: Tues-Fri, 10-5; Sat-Sun 11-5. Open Mon only during school holidays. Adults £4.50, Kids £4, Family of four £16.*

This museum was developed to stimulate kids' natural interest in storytelling and imagination. Kids can dress up, make puppets, tell and record their own stories, and explore fun areas that include a Secret Cave, Magic Parcel, Alien Spacebaby, and a vehicle known as the Lollipopter. The Story Garden outside features wacky activities, such as a monster whose tongue is a slide, and fun objects like boats, space ships, and cars for kids to go on their own great imaginary adventures.

18. THAMES RIVER & LONDON BRIDGE

The Thames is 215 miles long. Over the years, it has been a highway for great sailing ships, a source of drinking water for the city, and a smelly open sewer. Today, thanks to environmental awareness and efforts, the Thames is one of the cleanest urban rivers in the world. It hosts over 115 species of fish, as well as a huge population of water birds. It is a source of great pride, commerce, recreation, and beauty.

London Bridge. *Spans the river between the city's financial district and its thriving South Bank/Southwark neighborhoods. Tube: London Bridge or Monument.*

Although London Bridge is not much to look at today, it has a great history. The original bridge was built by the Romans during their occupation of Britain in the 1st century AD. It was a wooden structure built on floating pontoons, and was the first span ever built across the River Thames. It remained the city's only bridge until the early 1700s. A stone bridge was constructed starting in 1176. It took 30 years to complete and became a neighborhood onto itself with shops and houses. On either end stood a huge gate with defensive walls and crenellations. The southern gate was used to display the severed heads of condemned traitors, which were preserved in tar and mounted on stakes as a warning. Public stocks and a prisoner's cage were also displayed on the bridge.

The narrow arches of the medieval London Bridge (19 in all) acted as a partial dam and slowed the flow of the river. As a result, the Thames froze

over more often during the cold winter months. When the ice thickened, Londoners would set up Frost Fairs on the river with food stands, games, theaters, and even barbershops. These lasted until the early 1800s, when a new London Bridge was constructed with wider arches that let the river flow more rapidly (*see painting on previous page*). That bridge was sold to an American millionaire in the 1960s. He had the entire bridge dismantled, transported piece by piece, and reinstalled near his home in Lake Havasu, Arizona. The London Bridge you see today dates from 1973. It's main advantage is that it is a good way to get to the attractions on the south side of the River Thames. One other feature, for fans of Charles Dickens' *Oliver Twist* are the small steps going down on the SW side of London Bridge (by a building called Hibernia Chambers). They are known as "Nancy's Steps", and mark the site where her character is killed by the evil Bill Sikes for helping Oliver to escape the life of a thief.

London Dungeon. *28/34 Tooley Street, SE1. Right by the London Bridge Tube Station. Open daily 10-6 (Apr-Sep); extended hours until 9 Mon-Wed (Jul-Aug); 10:30-5:30 (Oct-Mar). Adults: £22.50, Kids: £16.50, Family of 4: £72. You can save some money and avoid queues by booking online in advance (www.the-dungeons.co.uk/london/en/tickets-prices/tickets-and-prices.htm)*

This museum is devoted to the gruesome side of London's past. For those of us who don't like things that go bump in the night, it's best to avoid this museum of horrors, appropriately housed in underground cellars on the South Bank of the Thames. But for those of you who love nothing better than a good haunted house, this a quite a treat. Many kids will consider it the highlight of their London trip.

There are more than 40 realistic exhibits (some with real actors) that take you through the Black Plague, Jack the Rippers' murders, the Great Fire of London, the Torture Chamber, the burning of witches, and other similar delights. There's a lot of blood and gore. Many parts are interactive with figures jumping out at you suddenly and judges putting you on trial. Consider yourselves warned – enjoy it at your own risk..

Britain at War Experience. *64-66 Tooley Street. SE1. Tube: London Bridge. Open daily 10-5:30 (Apr-Sep), 10-4:30 (Oct-Mar). Adults*

£13, kids 5-15 £5.50, family (2 adults + 2 kids) £29, Kids under 5 free.

This is another opportunity, along with the Cabinet War Rooms and Imperial War Museum, to see and feel life in London during the bombing Blitz of World War II. Special effects highlight the sights, sounds, smoke, and smells of wartime London life. It's very realistic, interactive, and designed to interest children. There is a subway air raid shelter, an Anderson shelter (that people erected in their back yards), a wartime GI club, a theater dressing room, a bomb disposal exhibit, and street full of shops. It's an important lesson for children about the reality of war, but may be too much for sensitive kids.

Hays Galleria. *Bankside, SE1. Located between Tower Bridge and London Bridge on the South Bank.*

This lovely, glass-covered shopping gallery is located on the site of the former Hays Wharf. It is here that the great tea clippers and other ships used to unload perishable foods for the city when the wharf was known as the "Larder of London". Today, people come to grab a bite to eat at one of the numerous cafés and restaurants, including the ubiquitous Starbucks. In the center of the gallery you can admire the whimsical nautical sculpture, with its moving pieces and squirting water. There's also a petanque pitch, if you like to play the French game of boules. Hays is a good place to eat after a visit to the Tower of London, Tower Bridge, or the HMS Belfast.

HMS Belfast. *Morgan's Lane, Tooley Street SE1. Moored between Tower Bridge and London Bridge, and by Hays Galleria. Tube: London Bridge. Open daily, 10-6 (summer), 10-5 (winter). Adults: £13, Kids under 16: free, but must be with an adult. There is a Kids Activity Guide and family-friendly activities on board throughout the year. Note: as of the writing of this book, some parts of the ship were closed for renovation.*

This 11,500-ton cruiser served with distinction during WWII and was part of the D-Day landing. It also served in the Korean War and Falklands War. Today it is a floating museum piece. You can visit all the decks and get a feel for life aboard from the numerous exhibits, above and below deck. Special family learning activities are often offered on weekends.

River Cruises. *Along the Thames, especially along Westminister Pier.*

Boat rides are often a hit with kids, and they offer you a chance to see some of the city's most beautiful sights from a unique vantage point. It's also a good solution for flat-footed tourists who balk at the idea of another long walk. Longer rides can be part of a great day-trip out of the city to Henry VIII's palace at Hampton Court or for a day of discovery in Greenwich.

Boat Races & River Events

The English take their crew races seriously, and two of the biggest crew races take place on the Thames. The **Head of the Thames** takes place in March and features hundreds of crews racing over a 4 mile course from Mortlake (SW14) to Putney (SW15). The **Oxford and Cambridge Boat Race** takes place in early April. These great rivals have been racing their dark blue and light blue teams for 150 years. The race goes from Putney to Mortlake. Spectators line up along the river. One strategy is to watch from the midway point at Hammersmith Tube.

In mid-July there is an event along the Thames called **Swan Upping**, where young cygnets are rounded up and tagged as property of the Queen, Vintners Guild, or Dyers Corporation. The Royal Swan Upping crew, led by the Royal Swanherd, goes up the River Thames to Henley. The young swans are marked according to their parents: one nick for those belonging to the Dyers, two for the Vintner's, and no nicks for those belonging to the Queen.

The **Doggett's Coat and Badge Race** takes place on or near August 1. This race unites professional watermen who race skiffs on a 5-mile course from London Bridge to Chelsea. The winners get prize money and a prize costume of red coat, breeches, and cap with white stockings and a silver medal.

September is the period of the **Great River Race** (*see photo below*) that attracts hundreds of boats of all types for a 23-mile course from Richmond, through London, and to Greenwich. There's also a spectacular waterfest at the end of September called the **Mayor's Thames Festival**. It features fun foods and activities, and an evening lantern procession followed by fireworks.

19. WATERLOO & LONDON EYE

This section of London offers lovely views from its riverside walks, not to mention spectacular vistas from the capsules of the London Eye.

London Eye. *Westminster Bridge Road, South Bank. Tube: Waterloo or Westminster. Ticket office located inside County Hall (directly next to the Eye). Open daily 9:30am-10pm (summer); 9:30-8 (winter). Regular fare - Adults: £17.50; Kids 5-15 £9.50; Kids under 5 free. You can save time and money by booking online in advance (www.londoneye.com). More expensive packages with souvenirs, drinks, and fast entry are available, too. You can also combine a ride on the London Eye with a River Cruise.*

The London Eye (*see photo on page 10 and below*) was built to celebrate the new millennium in 2000. It was meant to be temporary but has been such a hit that it's stuck around. Though it looks like one, it's not a ferris wheel, technically, because the capsules are enclosed and hang outside the wheel. Also the A-frame support holds the wheel from only one side. Still, the ride is terrific, even if you are afraid of heights. The London Eye is the 6th tallest structure in London, and from the top you can see up to 40 kilometers (25 miles) in each direction if the weather is clear – all the way to Windsor Castle and beyond. It contains 32 capsules, each with a capacity of 25 people. The Eye can transport as many as 15,000 people each day and

takes them on a 30-minute tour that goes 135 meters (450 feet) above the London skyline. No wonder the rides are called flights. Don't miss it!

London Eye River Cruise. *London Eye Pier. Daily departures every hour 11:45-6:45, Apr-Oct. Adults £12, Kids 5-15 £6; Kids under 4 free.*

This tour allows you to combine the birds-eye view of London's landmarks in the London Eye with a close-up view from the river. Cruises last 40 minutes and take you past St Paul's Cathedral, Houses of Parliament, Tower of London, HMS Belfast, Shakespeare's Globe, Tate Modern, and the Millennium bridge. There's a live commentary and free map. Boarding begins 15 minutes before departure time.

London Ducktours. *County Hall (By the London Eye). Tube: Waterloo. Phone: 020 7928 3132. Online: www.londonducktours.co.uk . Open daily. Tours last 70 minutes. Adults £20, Kids £14-16, depending on age, Families (2 adults + 2 kids) £58.*

The amphibious DUK boats were originally designed for the D-Day landings in WWII. With the Ducktours, they are used to take you around the major sights of the city by land, then splash into the Thames for a short river-view tour. It's a winning combination.

Sea Life London Aquarium. *South Bank across the Westminster Bridge. Open daily, 10-7, Fri-Sat, 10-8. Adults £18; Kids 3-14 £12.50; Family (2 adults, 2 kids) £55.*

The Sea Life Aquarium contains over 350 different species of fish, including eels, sharks, piranhas, rays, jellyfish, clownfish, tangs and many more. They are arranged in geographic zones, ranging from the deepest Atlantic to the warm waters of a coral reef. There are also exhibits on freshwater and pond fish, including Koi carp and fish with funny names like pumpkin seed and stickleback. A seashore exhibit lets visitors see and touch animals from the British sea coast, such as crabs, starfish, and anemones. There's also a large touch pool, where you can pet a thornback or spotted ray.

British Film Institute's IMAX Cinema. *1 Charlie Chaplin Walk, South Bank, (near the London Eye) SE1. Tube: Waterloo. Prices vary depending on movies and types of tickets. Standard price is Adults £8.50; Kids 4-14 £5.25; Kids under 4 free. Tickets are available at the box office; via phone: 0870 787 2525; and online (tickets.imax.bfi.org.uk).*

With 477 seats, this is the largest of London's IMAX theaters. The seats are tiered in such a way that even small children get a good view. The screen is over 20 meters high and 26 meters wide. There is an 11,600-watt digital surround-sound system. Some of the films are projected in 3-D vision.

Gabriel's Wharf. *56 Upper Ground and Riverside Walk, Southbank, London SE1 (by OXO Tower)*

This development features craft shops and cafés, arranged around a courtyard where bands play in the summer. The local community development group also organizes an annual Coin Street Festival (in early summer) here with free music, dance, and other performances.

Imperial War Museum. *Lambeth Road, SE1. Tube: Lambeth North or Elephant and Castle. Open daily, 10-65. Admission is free; charges for special exhibits. Audioguides are available for £3 at the Admissions Desk.*

Note: Ask for activity guides and special events at the front desk.

Originally designed as a memorial to those killed and wounded in World War I, this museum is dedicated to all the 20th century conflicts involving Britain and the British Commonwealth. It is full of warplanes, tanks, guns, and other military equipment. However, it also contains some very moving exhibits that describe the realities of war for soldiers and civilians. There are many hands-on exhibits, including a recreation of the Blitz, a World War I trench, and a house from the 1940s complete with an Anderson Bomb Shelter. Personal letters and testimonials give insights on battle life from the viewpoint of ordinary soldiers. There is a section on military espionage and on great escapes. Upstairs in the art galleries are some remarkable paintings from both World Wars, including John Singer Sargent's 1919 masterpiece *Gassed*, that depicts a line of men blinded by mustard gas in WWI. The top two floors of the museum are devoted to the Holocaust and to Crimes Against Humanity, but the exhibits are not

recommended for children under age 14.

The museum's building has an interesting history, too. It was built by James Bedlam in the early 1800s, and served for many decades as London's main insane asylum, known as Bedlam or Saint Mary's Bethlehem Hospital.

The **museum café**, located on the ground floor, offers freshly cooked food made from organic ingredients, including a Children's Menu.

20. SOUTH BANK

Settlers were fishing and trading on the South Bank of the Thames long before the Roman's invaded and created their city of Londonium. Even after London was established this area remained outside of the city's gates (and laws). In medieval days it was a bustling place where great sailing ships came to unload food and livestock. In Elizabethan times the South Bank was home to the city's theaters and bear-baiting arenas. Today, the neighborhood has been revived with the rebuilt Globe Theatre, soaring Tate Modern Museum, and fun places to eat and visit.

Note: There is a **tourist information center** inside the Vinopolis Building, 1 Bank End, SE1. Tube: London Bridge. Along with information on the neighborhood and rest of London, there are restrooms and a baby changing station.

Globe Theater. *21 New Globe Walk, Bankside, SE1. On the South bank of the Thames, across the Millennium Bridge from St Paul's Cathedral. Tube: London Bridge, Mansion House, or Blackfriars. Theater Tours and Exhibition are open daily 10-5 (Oct-Apr); 9-12 and 12:30-5 (May-Sep). During matinee*

performances visitors will see the Rose Theater down the street. Adults £10.50; Kids 5-15 £6.50; Family (up to 2 adults & 3 children) £20. For tickets to a theatrical performance visit or call the box office at: 020 7401 9919 or go online to www.shakespeares-globe.org.

Opened in 1599, the original Globe Theatre was an open-air playhouse where William Shakespeare worked and produced many of his plays. It was an integral part of the lively theatre scene on London's South Bank until it was forced to close (along with all of the city's theaters and bear-baiting arenas) by the Puritans in 1642. The Globe never reopened. Instead it fell into disrepair, was pulled down, and was replaced with tenement housing.

In 1949, the Hollywood actor and director Sam Wanamaker launched an effort to rebuild the Globe, when the only trace he could find of it was a plaque on a brewery wall. It was slow going for decades, but in 1989 the theater's original foundations were uncovered, and in 1992 work finally began on a reconstruction of the original theater. The New Globe was partially complete in 1993 for a production of *The Merry Wives of Windsor* celebrating Shakespeare's Birthday. It opened its first official season in April 1997, in the presence of HM Queen Elizabeth II and Prince Philip, who is Patron of the Shakespeare Globe Trust.

Seeing a Show. Today, the Globe offers a unique opportunity to experience theater as it was produced in Shakespeare's day. Known as the "Wooden O", it is shaped like a doughnut, with a covered stage on one end, and an open-air "Yard" in the middle surrounded by three levels of covered, wooden galleries.

When Shakespeare was writing and acting, as many as 500 theater goers would stand in the Yard, hooting and hollering at jokes, and throwing fruits or vegetables at the actors if they didn't like the show. The casts were entirely made up of male actors, with young men playing the female parts, as women were not allowed to perform on the stage. Today the casts consist of male and female actors, and occasionally as a twist, the theater will produce a play with an all-women cast.

For kids who are interested in seeing a live play, the Globe is a great place to do so. The stated policy of the Theater is that "children are especially welcome to watch performances". Thanks to the design of the building, you have the freedom to walk around from the seats in the galleries to the central Yard for a stage-level view of the play. You can also eat and drink in the theater, or come and go as needed. The performances generally last about 3 hours with a 20-minute intermission. We took a 1-hour break during one show, had dinner down the street, and returned to enjoy the last hour of the play.

Performances of Shakespeare's works, and those of his contemporaries, are offered from May to September. You can buy tickets for seats in the gallery or to stand as a "groundling" in the central Yard as common folk did 400 years ago (prices vary). This is an inexpensive option if you want your kids to experience some real Shakespeare but don't expect them to last through a whole performance.

Touring the Theater. Guided visits of the Globe are open all year and full of interactive displays and live demonstrations. You'll see how costumes are made and fitted, and get a chance to try on some Elizabethan armor. You may catch a sword fight or hear Shakespearean music on instruments of his era. You'll learn how actors can fly on the stage, and how the theater creates thunder, blood, and other special effects. On days when matinee shows are taking place, you won't get to go into the performance space, but will be taken instead to see the archeological remains of a sister theater called the **Rose** (see below).

Special events: From April to October, the Globe offers special workshops and activities. Some are specifically geared for families.

The Rose Theatre Exhibition. *56 Park Street, London SE1. Open daily, 10-5. Adults £7.50; Kids 5-15 £4.50; Kids under 5 free.*

Like the Globe, this is an Elizabethan-era theater that produced plays by Shakespeare and his contemporaries. It was also closed by the Puritans in 1606 and abandoned. The foundations were discovered in 1989 by archeologists. Knowledge gained from this excavation was used in the rebuilding of the Globe. Today the Rose Theater visit features a sound and lights show. It brings to life not only the history of the Rose Theatre but also the whole lively theatrical scene of the South Bank during Shakespeare's time.

Millennium Bridge. *Spans the river between Saint Paul's Cathedral and the Tate Modern and Globe Theater on the South Bank. Tube: Blackfriars or Saint Paul.*

This very modern-looking pedestrian bridge was opened in 2000 to celebrate the new millennium. Structural problems forced it to be quickly closed again, as it began to sway when too many people walked on it. Things were quickly set right and the bridge was reopened – although the repair bill was about £5 million.

Borough Market. *8 Southwark Street SE1. Located behind Southwark Cathedral, under the elevated train tracks. Tube: London Bridge. Open Fri 12-6 and Sat 9-4.*

This market has been around for 1000 years. Today, it is known for its high quality foods, including gourmet stalls that sell everything from imported wines and olives to delicious meat pies and pastries. It is a fun place to pick up a breakfast, lunch, or snack. Remember though that it's only open to the general public on Fridays and Saturdays.

The rest of the week it serves as an early morning wholesale market for local shops and restaurants.

Southwark Cathedral. *By Thames Walk and London Bridge, SE1.*

Southwark Cathedral is the oldest remaining Gothic church in London, most of it dating from the years 1220 to 1420. There are vestiges of Roman pavement in the floor left over from the beginning of the first millennium when this spot held a Roman Villa. The church also bears a few remains of a monastery – including a doorway in the north aisle of the nave – that stood here during the reigns of Edward the Confessor (1042-1066) and William the Conqueror (1066-).

Today, the inside of the cathedral contains a monument and window to William Shakespeare; a memorial to the 51 people who died in the 1989 boating accident of the Marchioness; a Tablet to Sam Wanamaker (American actor/producer who helped rebuild the Globe Theater); a St. Andrew's Chapel dedicated to those affected by HIV/AIDS; and a chapel named for John Harvard, founder of Harvard University.

In the visitors' center there is a camera that shows you the panoramic view of London from the top of the Cathedral's tower, and one that shows you scenes of Southwark. In the Refectory, you can grab a nice breakfast, lunch, or afternoon snack. If the weather permits you can enjoy them on the quiet outdoor terrace, near interesting sights such as the London Dungeon, *Golden Hinde*, and Globe Theatre, but removed from the hustle and bustle.

Golden Hinde. *St. Marie Overie Dock, Cathedral Street, SE1. Just east*

of the Globe Theatre and west of London Bridge. Tube: Monument or London Bridge. Adults £6; Kids 4-13 £4.50; Family £18. Open daily, 10-5:30, unless it is reserved for a special group or party.

This is a full-size reconstruction of the ship that was sailed around the world by Sir Frances Drake. It is very true to the original, down to the tiniest details, and gives a real feel for (the cramped) life on board a 16th century flagship. Actors in Elizabethan costumes help bring the experience to life further. The visit is very kid friendly. There are lots of special activities from pirate days to overnight stays where kids dress up in period costumes, eat hard biscuits, and try out their seafaring skills.

Tate Modern Museum. *Bankside, London (by the South side of the Millennium Bridge). Tube: Southwark or Blackfriars. Special Tate boats run every 40 min between Tate Britain, London Eye, and Tate Modern. Open Sun-Thur 10-6; Fri-Sat 10-10. Admission is free (donations encouraged). Special exhibits may require a fee. Audioguide rentals: £5 available at the Audio Tour Desks, Turbine Hall and Level 5.*

Note: There is a special **Children's Audio Guide Tour**; **Exhibition Trails**, based on temporary exhibits; and **Explorer Trails** for the permanent exhibits.

This museum houses the Tate collection of modern art dating from 1900 to the present. It is located in the former Bankside Power Station, and uses the vast spaces and windows overlooking the river to great advantage. The collection includes many major works by artists such as Dali, Duchamps, Giacometti, Picasso, Matisse, and Mondrian. There are also many pieces from more contemporary artists such as Rothko, Pollock, Warhol, and Gilbert and George. They are organized by themes rather than by style or chronology. The kids' trails and tours are really well done, and they will help your child explore and appreciate the whimsy and multiple meanings of modern art.

21. DOCKLANDS

In the 19th century this area, stretching east from Tower Bridge to the Millennium Dome in N. Greenwich, bustled with shipping traffic. Rum, sugar, and hardwoods were delivered at the West India Docks, while exotic spices and silks came through the East India Docks. Wool and rubber were delivered to St. Katharine's Docks; ivory, coffee, and cocoa were unloaded at Wapping. There was also an important shipbuilding industry in the London Docklands, attracting many ironworkers, carpenters, and other craftsmen.

During World War II, the docks were heavily damaged by German bombardments and by the late 1950s they were outmoded due to the introduction of deep-water container ships. Two decades of redevelopment, and the expansion of public transportation access with the Docklands Light Railroad and prolongation of the Jubilee tube line, have breathed new life into the area.

Wapping. *Located between St. Katherine's Dock and the Isle of Dogs.*
This area is most famous as the site where pirates were put to death in the 19th century. The method was pretty simple: pirates were tied up and placed in such a way that the rising river tides would drown them (*see photo on next page*). Their bodies would be left there during three consecutive high tides to serve as a warning to others.

Isle of Dogs. This area once housed royal dog kennels and still features domesticated animals at **Mudchute City Farm** on Pier Street (Docklands Light Railroad Mudchute Station). Entrance is free and there are special activities during school holidays

The **Greenwich and Docklands International Festival** is held on the Isle of Dogs and across the river in Greenwich in early July. It features music, theater, and other art demonstrations.

A pedestrian tunnel goes under the Thames to link the southern tip of the Isle of Dogs with Greenwich.

Museum in Docklands. *No. 1 Warehouse, West India Quay, Hertsmere Road, London, E14. Open daily, 10-6. Entrance is free. There are free family events on Saturdays and during school vacations.*

The Museum in Docklands is located in the former spice, rum, and cotton warehouses of the West India Quay. It is modern and very kid friendly. There is a whole section specially devoted to children, with lots of hands-on activities. Kids can learn about the history of the river and shipping by playing with winches, balancing cargo, weighing goods, looking for archeological relics in the Foreshore Discovery box, or tracing cargo to its country of origin on an interactive map. One section recreates the streets and alleys of 19th century Wapping. Others focus on archeological finds, scale models of the docks, and the people who worked there. The museum also has full-scale models of boats and real vessels moored by the West India Dock.

22. GREENWICH

Greenwich is famous for its location as the Prime Meridian, the spot from which all international time and longitude are measured. However, Greenwich is much more, too. When Britain ruled the seas, Greenwich was its seafaring hub and home to the Royal Naval College. Today, Greenwich sports a wonderful Maritime Museum, and it's where you can visit a real clipper ship, see a small boat that broke a world record, and take a boat ride of your own on the Thames. Finally, it is home to the bucolic Greenwich Park and charming shopping streets of old Greenwich Village.

Getting There: Greenwich is located five miles down river from central London. You can go by tube on the Jubilee Line to the North Greenwich station or take the Docklands Light Railway to the Cutty Sark station. If you are coming from the Isle of Dogs, you can take the 100-year-old foot tunnel under the Thames from the Island Gardens to Greenwich. For a slower ride and fun adventure, go by boat from Westminster Pier, Charing Cross Pier, or Tower Pier. Boats leave every 30 minutes or so and the ride takes 30-40 minutes, depending on where you depart in London.

Royal Observatory. *Greenwich Park. London SE10. Open daily 10-5. Admission is free.*

The Royal Obervatory was founded by King Charles II in 1675. It was built out of old ship timbers and bricks that had been recuperated from demolished parts from the Tower of London. Charles II appointed John

Flamsteed as Royal Astronomer and gave him the task of establishing a way for sailing ships to measure their east-west position when out of sight of land. Flamsteed observed the motions of the stars and set up a way to calculate longitude, using Greenwich as the zero degree point. King

Charles also recruited Christopher Wren, who was both an astronomer and an architect, to design the building.

In 1960, the official Royal Observatory was transferred to Herstmonceux and later Cambridge, because pollution from London was obscuring the observations. The building still contains the largest refractor telescope (28-inches) in the world. The telescope was built in 1893 and collects light through lenses rather than mirrors. It weighs 1.4 tons. Amazingly, the observatory dome was originally made of paper-maché. However bombing damage destroyed it during World War II, and it was replaced with a dome made of fiberglass.

Inside the Royal Observatory you can see historic astronomical instruments; set your watch to the exact Greenwich Mean Time by the observatory's digital clock; look for the brass Meridian Line; or check out the time on the 24-hour clock. The Observatory also has an interesting camera obscura – a dark room where you see an image of the view from the observatory reflected through a lens in the roof. From the terraces around the observatory there are also excellent views of Greenwich Park, the Thames, the Docklands, and in the distance, downtown London.

If you look at the roof of the Royal Observatory and you will notice a spire that holds a red ball. Every day the ball slides down the rod at exactly 1 pm. It was installed in 1883 so that sailors and clockmakers could set their timepieces. There is another interesting timepiece on the observatory wall: it's a 24-hour clock.

Prime Meridian Line. *Runs through the Royal Observatory. Look for the brass marker on the ground.*

The Meridian is an imaginary line running from the North to the South Pole on both sides of the globe, from which time and longitude are measured. Until the late 19th century, there were numerous, competing meridian lines, including at least nine in England and one in Paris. The Greenwich Meridian became the established Prime Meridian worldwide at an International Meridian Conference held in Washington DC in 1884. Countries from around the world agreed that the mean solar day would begin at midnight in Greenwich, and universal time and longitude would be measured from there in positive increments towards the east and negative ones towards the west. The Greenwich Meridian is also known as the International Date Line.

The meridian line provides a great **photo opportunity**. Stand on the brass line and you are at exactly 0 degrees longitude. Straddle the line and you will have a foot on each side of the world: one in the eastern hemisphere and the other in the western hemisphere.

The observatory has a **planetarium**, which offers a variety of different shows on stars, planets, and the universe.

National Maritime Museum. *Romney Road, Greenwich, London SE10. Open daily, 10-5. Admission is free.*

Note: An **explorer's trail** for kids 6-11 is available at the entrance. Turn it in at the end of your visit and you'll get a treat. The **all-hands gallery** is filled with interactive exhibits designed for kids. **Shipmates activities** are set up with displays for more hands-on enjoyment. **Audioguides** are avail-

able for certain exhibits. **Family-friendly activities**, such as a paper boat-making workshop, are offered on Sundays – check the schedule.

This fun museum features many relics and stories from Britain's seafaring past – going all the way back to the Vikings. There are full size weapons, uniforms, ship models and more. There are lots of multi-media exhibits and hands-on activities that captivate the interests of kids and parents alike. Exhibits give you a feel for life on board a 19th century warship, modern naval frigate, or luxurious ocean liner. You can admire a royal barge, look at a Greenpeace capsule, or check out a cat-'a-nine-tails. You can see how a sailing ship is rigged, try to communicate with signal flags, sink a ship with a torpedo, steer a Viking longboat, or look for the hole in Admiral Nelson's uniform made by the French bullet that killed him in the Battle of Trafalgar.

Cutty Sark. *Cutty Sark Gardens, King William Walk, Greenwich, London SE 10. Open daily, 10-5. Entrance is free.*

Note: The ship caught fire in 2007 and visits to the ship are suspended until repair work is concluded.

The *Cutty Sark* is a real clipper ship, launched in 1869. The clippers were famous for their speed (they could outrun steam ships if the wind was blowing) and the *Cutty Sark's* streamlined shape made her one of the fastest. Her original aim was to bring back tea from China at a rapid clip. Indeed she broke a shipping record of the day, covering 363 miles in 24 hours. However, shortly after her first voyages, the Suez Canal was completed allowing steamer ships to reach the Far East faster than the sailing ships, which could not go through the canal. The *Cutty Sark* then became famous for transporting wool to Britain from Australia in record times. However, by the 1890s that business was no longer lucrative, the ship fell out of use, and became quite delipadiated. It was restored in the 1950s and was undergoing new renovations when it caught fire in 2007.

Gypsy Moth IV. *Open Apr-Oct, Mon-Sat 10-6, Sun 12-6.*

This is the 53-foot craft in which Francis Chichester sailed single-handedly around the world in 1966. He set a new world record of 274 days, beating those established by the old clipper ships. He was knighted by Queen Elizabeth II on his return to England. She used the same sword with which Queen Elizabeth I had knighted Sir Francis Drake in 1582.

Heading downstream from the *Cutty Sark* and *Gypsy Moth* you can stroll along the **Five Foot Walk** (measure the width and you'll see where the name comes from). It leads to the Trafalgar Tavern – a favorite of both Charles Dickens and contemporary Londoners.

Greenwich Palace (now the Royal Naval College Buildings) and the Queen's House. *Greenwich Park. SW10.*

The original Greenwich Palace was built by King Henry VII and was a favorite home of the Tudor royals. The Queen's house was built later and completed in 1635. It served as a model for the White House in Washington DC and is said to be haunted by a woman in white.

Greenwich Park. Greenwich was called *Grenewic* by the Saxons, meaning Green Village, and that bucolic heritage lives on in Greenwich Park. The park offers terrific views and great places for kids to frolic. There's a lake where you can rent canoes and rowboats. There is a playground and spaces where locals come to fly kites. There are also tennis courts, a putting green, fields where you can watch a rugby or cricket match, and a children's boating pool. There is a large grassy enclosure covering 12 acres where deer, foxes, and many birds run wild. A bandstand offers concerts on Sundays and throughout the summer. Check out the dolphin sundial in the Titanic Garden, and the hollow old oak trunk in which Queen Elizabeth I is said to have taken tea when she was young and living in the Greenwich Palace.

Greenwich Village. The side streets of Greenwich are well worth exploring, including Greenwich Church Street, Greenwich High Road, King William Walk, College Approach, Nelson Road, and Turnpin Lane. They feature maritime souvenirs, antiques, flower venders, food markets, flea markets, and an arts and crafts market. Weekends are especially busy.

23. HAMPSTEAD

This neighborhood's famous park, Hampstead Heath, served as the inspiration for author C.S. Lewis' make-believe world of evil witches, talking animals, and heroic princes and princesses described in his *Chronicles of Narnia* series. The woodlands and meadows do lend themselves to kids' adventures, with deer, graceful water birds, fishing and boating, swimming ponds, and lots of family-friendly summer entertainment.

Hampstead Village. *Located 4 miles N of central London. Tube: Hampstead, Hampstead Heath, or Golders Green.*

Hampstead Village is dotted with pretty lanes, rose-covered gardens, and lovely Georgian and Regency era houses. There's fun shopping (including toy stores) along the pedestrian Flask Walk. Heath Street and High Street offer shops, tea houses, and restaurants.

Hampstead Heath. *Located 4 miles NW of central London. Tube: Hampstead.*

This vast park is very popular with Londoners who come for a breath of fresh air and chance to enjoy the pleasures of the great outdoors. There are playgrounds, tennis courts, areas filled with birds and deer, and plenty of room to run. In the summer months you can see fairs, concerts, and theatrical performances or go for a swim in one of the pools. You can watch the model boats maneuver around the Boating Pond or see if anything is catching in one of the fishing ponds. Parliament Hill offers good views of London, fine sledding if it's snowy, and excellent kite flying.

24. CASTLE IN THE COTSWOLDS!

We should subtitle this bonus excursion, after Monty Python, *And Now for Something Completely Different!* Note that this chapter was written by Jonathan Stein, publisher of Open Road's travel guide series.

Thornbury Castle: A Castle-Hotel Filled with History!

Some boosters have called this incredible destination "the best hotel in Europe."

If you have the time, consider taking a break from London and staying for a few days in the lovely western Cotswolds, not far from the border with Wales. Kids of all ages, I think it's fair to say, will enjoy staying in a castle-hotel: 500-year old **Thornbury Castle**, less than a two-hour train ride due west from London. Thornbury is now the only remaining Tudor castle in England serving as a hotel.

The hotel is outside the city of Bristol in the town of Thornbury, and is dripping with history. Henry VIII and Anne Boleyn once stayed here, in what is now called the Duke's Bedchamber. There are vineyards on the vast grounds where the castle's wine is still produced, and some of the oldest and prettiest Tudor gardens in England are here too:

We stayed in the Portlethen Suite, which has a four-poster bed, a jacuzzi, ornate wood panelling and medieval-style wall tapestries. My daughter asked if our suite had its own ghost too: If it did, the apparition was hard to see or hear!

All told there are 27 guest rooms and suites in the castle, each with their own style and furnishings, each unique, most with fireplaces. A few even have arrow-slit windows for you to help defend the keep! The accommodations are lovely and comfortable (*see photo, next page, top*).

Thornbury has an excellent reputation for its restaurant, and we can attest that it's well-deserved.. The chef and dining room have won a number of awards, and the ingredients are local. The Tudor Dining Hall, dating from the 16th century, with its suits of armor, huge hearth, and stone walls, is available for private functions. What a fun room!:

If you're not arranging a private dinner, you'll dine either in the Oriel Room or the Tower Dining Room, an elegant octagonal room with those arrow-slit windows and a great big roaring fire. In addition to the castle's own wine there is an extensive international wine list. Thornbury Castle is the recipient of *The Wine Spectator's* 'Award of Excellence.'

After dinner, go down to one of the sitting rooms for a drink and dessert. You can have story time here from one of the old classics that fill the bookshelves in these wonderful rooms. Nothing like a little *Beowulf* from the old Anglo-Saxon word-hoard to ease your child's transition to bedtime!

The gardens are superb, a great way for you to relax and your kids to run around exploring. Croquet, archery, clay pigeon shooting and falconry are all available on-site (the latter two with prior notice and at an extra

charge). Fishing and biking and other activities can be arranged off-site.

Thornbury Castle also has its own vineyard, used to make Thornbury wines. If you are here during harvest time, you and your children can participate in grape picking.

The castle is close to

Wales, and not far from nearby ruins, market towns in the Cotswolds, the old Roman town of Bath; and even Stonehenge is within driving distance.

During our visit we spent an incredibly beautiful, misty, drizzly day among the nearby ruins at **Tintern Abbey** in Wales (*photo below*). If you get a chance, see this Abbey, one of the greatest monastic ruins in all of Wales. The Cistercian order flourished here from the 12th century until the plague (Black Death) struck in 1348. The order remained, however, until Henry VIII order the destruction of the monasteries in 1536. The poetically-minded among you may know that William Wordsworth penned *Lines Written A Few Miles Above Tintern Abbey* in 1798, which begin:

Five years have past; five summers, with the length
Of five long winters! and again I hear
These waters, rolling from their mountain-springs
With a sweet inland murmur. — Once again
Do I behold these steep and lofty cliffs...

We used Thornbury to explore part of Wales, but it's a fine base for those wishing to see the ancient Roman ruins at Bath or the western part of the Cotswolds. It's a beautiful area. If you're looking to see another part of England during a London trip – including the option of staying in the largest bed in all of Great Britain! – then check out one-of-a-kind Thornbury Castle.

25. BEST SLEEPS & EATS

Food and lodging can be expensive in London, with some unpleasant surprises. If you want a clean, modern hotel, it's a good idea to stick to the large, well-known chains. We've also tried to find some more traditional hotels that offer family-friendly advantages, such as kitchenettes or family suites. Regarding restaurants, you can generally find decent and affordable pizza places and Indian restaurants to takeout or eat in.

There are also lots of sandwich shop chains, along with chains like **Patisserie Valerie** and **Café Rouge,** which pride themselves on being kid friendly and have locations around the city. **Ed's Easy Diners** or **My Old Dutch Pancake House** are also good bets.

THE CITY

Citadines-Barbican Apartment/Hotel. *21 Goswell Road, Barbican. EC1. Tube: Barbican. Tel. +44 (0)20 7566 8000. Rooms start at £200 for a 1-bedroom apartment that sleeps 4. www.citadines.com/uk/london/barbican.html.*

These modern apartments are situated in a 7-story building that is located close to the Museum of London and St. Paul's Cathedral. They lack old-world charm, but make up for it in comfort, convenience, and reliability – each 1-bedroom unit has a kitchenette (fridge, microwave, hotplate, coffeemaker), dining area, safe, TV, full bathroom with hairdryer, bedroom with double bed, and living room with a pull-out double bed.

Note: you can also rent two studio apartments with an adjoining door. Linens and towels are provided. It's a great solution for families.

Museum of London Cafés. *150 London Wall, EC2, Tube: Barbican or St. Pauls.*

The museum offers several family-friendly cafés. There are kids' box lunches with sandwich, drink, fruit, dessert, and a toy. Kids can also order a child-size portion from the regular hot course selections.

The Place Below at St. Mary Le Bow Church. *Crypt. St. Mary Le Bow, the City, EC2. Tube: St Paul's.*

This place, in the 11th century crypt of a church designed by Christopher Wren, serves home-made fare for lunch and dinner. Features include quiches, salads, breads, soups, hot dishes, and desserts. They are open for breakfast, lunch, and dinner.

TRAFALGAR SQUARE

Citadines-Trafalgar. *18-21 Northumberland Avenue, Trafalgar Square. WC2. Tel. 020 7766 3700 Tube: Charing Cross or Embankment. Rooms start at £200 for 1- and 2-bedroom apartments. www.citadines.com/uk/london/ trafalgar_square.html*

This apartment/hotel is wonderfully located between the Thames and Trafalgar Square. It is close to many of the central London sights that you'll want to see with your kids, such as the horse guard, Nelson's Column, St. Martin's in the Fields Church, the National Gallery and National Portrait Gallery, Big Ben, Westminster Abbey, St. James Park, the Cabinet War Rooms, and much more. It offers both 1-bedroom apartments that can accommodate 4 people and 2-bedroom duplex apartments that can accommodate a family of 6. If you are traveling with a baby you can request a crib (called a baby cot) and a changing pad. There is an indoor parking lot in the building. As with all the Citadines apartments you get a kitchenette (fridge, microwave, hotplate), dining area, safe, TV, full bathroom with hairdryer, sheets, towels, and a laundry service in the building.

Crypt Café, St. Martin's in the Fields Church. *Trafalgar Square. WC2. Tube: Charing Cross.*

This remains one of our favorite family-friendly eateries in London. It's good, easy, and affordable. You go down into the church crypt, with its arched ceilings and old stones. The food is served cafeteria style, but the ingredients are fresh and selection is wide. You can pick from hot dishes, salads, sandwiches, quiches, and the like. There are also pastries and snacks. When you are finished with your food, you can check out the Brass Rubbing Center where you can pick up a fun souvenir or make your own. Or for a musical treat, try to catch one of the free lunchtime concerts in the church upstairs. The café is open for breakfast, lunch, and dinner. There are jazz concerts on Thursday evenings in the crypt.

Café and Restaurant. *National Gallery. Trafalgar Square. WC2. Tube: Charing Cross.*

This is a great kid-friendly museum, and the café and restaurant also cater to kids with high chairs and children's menus.

Smollensky's on the Strand. *105 The Strand. WC2. Tube: Charing Cross.*

This place is very good with kids, especially on weekends when they have family lunches with live, kid-friendly entertainment. Smollensky's also does children's birthday parties. The menu is primarily American with big steaks, BBQ wings, hamburgers, and coleslaw. There are some non-meat options, as well. Kids can pick from their own menu. The cheesecakes and chocolate mousse are a big hit.

COVENT GARDEN

One Aldwych *1 Aldwych, WC2B 4BZ. Tube: Charing Cross or Holborn Station. Tel 020 7300 1000. Family ooms start at £395 but check for speicals. www.onealdwych.com.*

This hotel is a contemporary gem. Doesn't look contemporary, does it? In fact, the outside is a classic Edwardian building protected by English Heritage. Looks great to me! But wait 'til you see the inside. When you first step into the lobby, you can see the transformation from old London to new:

The location is excellent, near the Thames and within walking distance of great sights, shopping, museums and especially West End theater.

Each of the 105 rooms and suites boasts original art, and the hotel overall has more than 400 pieces of modern art and sculpture. As you'd expect, the look in each room is contemporary with all the amenities you could want, from freshly cut flowers, fruit, feather and down duvets, soft linens, CD players, and much more! Feast your eyes on this luxurious suite:

After a long day of touring, you can lounge around in a wonderful pool, get a variety of spa treatments, or work out in their gym. And after a dip in the pool – on weekends – enjoy a movie in their screening room!

The hotel's Axis Restaurant is wonderful, a modern affair. Try the braised beef bourguignon in red wine with mashed swede, carrots and baby onions, or the butternut squash risotto.

Upon arrival, your little ones will be treated to a welcome gift, and if you need extra beds for the kids that's no problem either. Children's bathrobes and slippers and babysitters are also available. Kids' menus in the restaurants, the pool, a movie room, a CD/games library – if you're traveling with kids, this is a great choice.

Renaissance Chancery Court Hotel. *252 High Holborn, WC1. Tube: Holborn Station. Tel. 020 7829 9888. Rooms start at £240. The Duck Package is £395 for a family of 4 for 2 nights. Check for other special offers. www.renaissancehotels.com/loncc.*

This is an upscale hotel that is part of the Marriott chain, with spacious rooms. They offer a special family package, called the Duck Package, which includes 2 nights' accommodations for a family of four, with full English breakfast, a trip on the London Duck Tour, special duck treats in the room, and duck packs for the kids. Adults get fluffy towels, nice toiletries, and complimentary coffee and tea. There is also a spa on site. Tea and scones are served in the afternoon.

Citadines-Covent Garden Apartment/Hotel. *94-99 High Holborn, Covent Garden. WC1. Tube: Holburn. Tel. 020 207 395 88 00. Rooms start at £180 for a 1-bedroom apartment that sleeps 4. www.citadines.com/en/uk/london/holborn_covent_garden.com*

These modern apartments are located in a 6-story building in the heart of central London. They lack old-world charm, but make up for it in comfort, convenience, and reliability – each 1-bedroom unit has air-conditioning, a kitchenette (fridge, microwave, hotplate), dining area, safe, TV, full bathroom with hairdryer, bedroom with double bed, and living room with a pull-out double bed. Linens and towels are provided. It's a great solution for families.

Fire & Stone Pizza Restaurant. *31-32 Maiden Lane, WC2. In Covent Garden. Tube: Covent Garden*

This place offers pizzas with toppings inspired by foods from around the world. There's also plenty of pasta and a kids menu for £5 that lets children build their own pizza or pasta plate, and choose from 5 drinks, and 3 types of ice cream for dessert.

The Crusting Pipe. *Located downstairs in Covent Garden, in the main market hall at 27 The Market, WC2. Tube: Covent Garden.*

Here, the tables are set under arched ceilings in an atmosphere that is cozy and intimate. Service is warm and friendly.

The menu is full of classic English comfort food, such as sausage, potatoes, ham, steak, chicken, and various salads. The kids' menu offered choices of bangers and mash, ham with potatoes and beans, or pasta. The adult selections give you choices of 1, 2, or 3 courses at reasonable prices.

Maxwells. *8 James Street. WC2. In Covent Garden. Tube: Covent Garden*

This restaurant is lively, kid-friendly, and in a great location. The kids' menu includes a main meal, soft drink, and dessert. The regular menu offers everything from a kids' club sandwich to fish fingers and fruit kebabs for dessert.

Neal's Yard World Food Café. *14 Neal's Yard. 1ˢᵗ floor. WC2. Tube: Covent Garden.*

Neal's Yard is an interesting little square, just west of Neal Street, which runs north from Covent Garden Market. The Yard is filled with organic eateries, includ-ing a bakery, salad bar, grocery, and this upstairs restaurant. The food is all vegetarian and organic, with lots of variety. You can choose a West African selection with bananas, peanuts, and sweet potatoes on rice, or Mexican, Indian, Turkish, and Middle-Eastern combos. There are also yummy desserts. Small kids might want to share a platter; portions are generous. They may enjoy sitting at the big U-shaped bar where you can watch the chefs in action. Make sure to visit the restrooms with their aquarium-style water tanks.

Belgo Centraal. *50 Earlham Street, WC2. Tel. 020 7813 2233. Tube: Covent Garden*

This is a fun restaurant. You enter by walking on a gangplank over the steaming kitchen, then go down the elevator to a place where the waiters are dressed up as monks. There are big refectory tables and also booths. The food is Belgian with plenty of steamed mussels, fries, and beer. But you can also opt for rotisserie chicken or duck, steaks, French specialties such as Confit de Canard (duck stew) and Bouchée aux Champignons (puff pastry filled with wild mushrooms). The kids' menu offers a main course and dessert for £5.

The Rock and Sole Plaice. *47 Endell Street, WC2. Tube: Covent Garden.*

This restaurant is conveniently located between Covent Garden and the British Museum. It is very popular, and we were surprised how many people they could fit in what looked like a small building. The best seating is outside if the weather is good. The specialty here is fish and chips – with numerous choices of fish. There are also other English specialties, such as Cornish pastie (meat pie), steak and kidney pie, mushy peas, and several custard-style desserts. For less adventurous palates there are basic choices such as hamburger or sausage.

Café-Patisserie Valerie. *8 Russell Street. WC2. Tel. 020 7240 0064. Tube: Covent Garden.*

This café and pastry shop has numerous locations around the city. This particular one is especially convenient for Covent Garden attractions. You can stop in for breakfast or a snack of delicious pastries, or go for a full meal. The mood is warm and cheery and you can choose from grilled sandwiches, burgers, salads, and the standard, "bangers and mash" – all at prices that won't break the bank.

Cornish Bakehouse. *James Street, WC2. Tube: Covent Garden.*

This takeout shop is located on a pedestrian street between the Covent Garden tube stop and the Market Halls. Here you have a choice of meat and vegetable filled pastries known as Cornish pasties. They make a good meal or snack for families on the go.

TGI Fridays. *6 Bedford Street, WC2. Tube: Covent Garden or Charing Cross.*

This is part of the family-friendly chain where you'll find familiar American selections, a kids' menu, and the requisite crayons and activity sheet. There are special deals for families. Little kids under 5 can choose from the Kinder Surprise menu. Organic baby food is also available.

PICADILLY CIRCUS/LEICESTER SQUARE

Brown's Hotel. *Albemarle Street, Mayfair, London W1S. Tube: Green Park or Piccadilly Circus. Tel. 020 7493 6020. Family packages start at £590 for a family of 4. Check for other specials. www.roccofortecollection.com.*

If you are looking for a luxury family getaway in the center of London, this is a good option. Brown's is clean, comfortable, and contemporary - even though it claims to be one of the first hotels in London. It's where Rudyard Kipling wrote *The Jungle Book*, and you are likely to find of copy of it, and other carefully chose classics, in your room. The hotel offers special family-friendly packages, for example offering two connecting

rooms for the price of one De-
luxe Room, with full English
breakfast for 2 adults and 2
children. Kids receive complimentary milk and cookies before bed. Those under 3 eat for
free, and kids under 12 pay half
price for meals. There are toys
and treats for the kids, special
themed children's linens, kiddie
bathrobes and slippers, and jun-

ior bathtime accessories. Babies get a crib, baby bed linen, a mobile, night
light, and changing facilities. Teens can play Wii, X-box and other games.
There are DVD players and a fitness center open to the family. There's also
a spa for the grownups.

Fortnum and Mason Food Hall. *Ground Floor. 181 Piccadilly, W1.
Tube: Piccadilly Circus or Green Park.*

This establishment has been providing ready-to-eat gourmet foods to
British Royalty and regular folks for over 100 years. You can find all sorts
of fancy foods, including the well-known jams and tarts, in the food hall
or head down to the lower level where they sell pre-stocked picnic hampers
for all sorts of occasions. There are also several restaurants to choose from,
for a fancy afternoon tea.

Popular American Chains: **Planet Hollywood.** *13 Coventry Street. W1.
Tel. Tube: Piccadilly Circus.* **Hard Rock Café.** *150 Old Park Lane, W1. Tel.
020 7514 1700. Tube: Green Park or Hyde Park Corner.* **Rainforest Café.** *20
Shaftesbury Avenue, W1. Tel. 020 7434 3111. Tube: Piccadilly Circus.*

These are perennial favorites with both British and American families.
You'll find the familiar settings and menus –a good option with homesick
kids or picky eaters.

Rock Island Diner. *London Pavillion. 1 Piccadilly, W1. Tel. Tube
Piccadilly Circus.*

This is yet another American-style eatery that kids enjoy. There's
1950s-style décor, dancing waiters, disco-music, and reasonable prices.

Stockpot Soho. *18 Old Compton Street, Soho. W1. Tube: Leicester
Square.*

This restaurant is part of the Stockpot chain that has several locations
in London. It's a great formula: good food, good prices, and friendly
service. They offer a choice of hearty hot plates, as well as pasta, salad, and
omelet selections. The one down side is that it can get crowded.

Pollo. 20 Old Compton Street, Soho. W1. Tube: Leicester Square.

As the name indicates, this restaurant specializes in chicken –cooked all sorts of different ways. However, there are also other choices, including numerous pasta dishes and vegetarian options. There's nothing fancy about this place, so families feel quite at ease. The prices are very reasonable, making this a popular and sometimes crowded locale.

HYDE PARK/KENSINGTON/KNIGHTSBRIDGE

The Athenaeum. *116 Piccadilly, Mayfair, London W1J. Tube: Green Park or Hyde Park. Tel. 020 7499 3464. Super family deals start at £200, including 5 hours of free babysitting. Check the website for rates and special packages. www.athenaeumhotel.com.*

This classy hotel is across from Green Park and a short walk to Hyde Park, Buckingham Palace, and Trafalgar Square. It offers a range of traditional and contemporary rooms, including connecting rooms and family friendly suites, some of which have kitchens and washing machines. There is a special concierge just for kids, and they have nannies available to babysit. Some nice touches include milk and cookies at bedtime for the kids, toys, and fruit at the check-in desk.

The Goring. *Beeston Place, SW1W 0JW. Tube: Victoria Station. Tel. 020 7396 9000. Rates start at £400, but seasonal specials are available. www.thegoring.com.*

Located just a few minutes from Buckingham Palace – and speaking of palaces, the hotel chosen by Kate Middleton to spend her final night as a commoner before she became (the future) Princess of Wales. Yes, it's that

grand a place, with impeccable service and style, yet not stuffy or over the top – and it is a superb family hotel choice.

Welcome goodies include among other fun items a Baaaa-bara sheep. If your child is game, you can set up an appointment in the kitchen, putting on an apron and chef's hat and baking cookies with the Chef at The Goring's wonderful restaurant – newly refurbished by Linley, one of England's premier furniture makers. Breakfast fare is hearty, delicious, and plentiful.

The 71 rooms and suites face either the hotel gardens or either Victoria Square or Beeston Place. Done up in classic English styles, each room is different yet each elegant. In addition to the usual amenities, you'll have on-demand films and music in the room's entertainment system, and high speed internet access as well. You can use the LA Fitness Club's pool, sauna and gym, just a three-minute walk from the hotel.

Milestone Hotel and Suites. *1 Kensington Court, London, W8. Tube: High Street Kensington. Tel. 020 7917 1000. Rates for family deals start at £370. www.milestonehotel.com.*

This luxury hotel is conveniently located across from Kensington Gardens. Though it is quite fancy, it caters specifically to kids and their families. They offer spe-cial beds and linens for kids, along with mini bath-robes and slippers. At bed-time, you'll find a teddy bear book and chocolate for the little ones. There is a kit of coloring books, pencils, movies, and games, and you can ask for baby strollers, high chairs, playpens, booster seats, and bottle warmers. There is an in-house nanny serv-

ice. The "We are Family" package includes family rooms with king and twin beds in adjacent rooms or suites. Older kids are invited for a special behind-the-scenes tour of the hotel, where they see different departments and meet the staff. They are even given a special "job" for which they get a special certificate.

Citadines-South Kensington Apartment/Hotel. *35A Gloucester Road. SW7. Tube: Gloucester Road. Tel. 020 7543 7878. Rates: £180 for a 1-bedroom that sleeps 4. www.citadines.com/en/uk/london/south_kensington.html,*

This apartment/hotel is located just steps from Hyde Park and the Natural History, Science, and Victoria/Albert Museums. It's a great location and very well connected to other parts of the city. The hotel was recently refurbished. 1-bedrooms apartments are set up as duplexes. Each has air-conditioning, a kitchenette (fridge, microwave, hotplate), dining area, safe, TV, full bathroom with hairdryer, bedroom with double bed, and living room with a pull-out double bed. Linens and towels are provided. There's a small fitness room in the building.

Fraser Place Queen's Gate. *39B Queens Gate Gardens,London SW7 Tube: Kensington. Tel. 020 7969 3555. Rooms range from studios to 2-bedrooms, with rates £160-300 per night, with reduced rates for multiple night stays. www.fraserplacequeensgate.com.*

This apartment-hotel offers the services of a hotel along with apartment conveniences, including a kitchenette furnished with dishes and cooking things, living area, cable TV with DVD, iron/ironing board. The bathrooms are spacious and stocked with L'Occitane products. There is a free washing machine in the building, and a self-service breakfast is included with the room rate. The location is also very handy to some of the great free, kid-friendly museums of London; Natural History, Science, and Victoria & Albert.

Number Sixteen. *16 Sumner Place.SW7. Tube: South Kensington. Tel. +44 (0) 20 7589 5232. Rates start at £150. www.firmdale.com/index.php?page_id=17.*

Part of the Firmdale Hotel Group, Number Sixteen is located in South Kensington, near the Museum of Science, Victoria & Albert Museum, Hyde Park, and shopping at Harrods. The 42 bedrooms offer comfort and an escape from the hustle and bustle of the city. For families, opt for two adjoining rooms and be sure to book afternoon tea in the outdoor garden.

Giraffe Restaurant. *7 Kensington High Street, London W8. Tube: High Street Kensington.*

This reasonably-priced restaurant is part of a chain offering kid-friendly fare for breakfast, lunch, and dinner. Breakfast choices include things like classic porridge with honey and strawberries, or stacks of pancakes with banana and blueberries, bagel with smoked salmon and eggs, or full brunch with sausage, bacon, and beans. For lunch and dinner there are lots of healthy salads, burgers, enchiladas, pizza, stir fry, falafel, and more. For early diners, there are special happy hour menu prices from 5-7 pm.

Sticky Fingers. *14 Phillimore Gardens, London, W8. Tube: High Street Kensington.*

If the name reminds you of an old Rolling Stones album, it's because this restaurant was founded by the band's bass player, Bill Wyman. The walls offer Stones memorabilia and the menu has plenty of kid-friendly choices such as burgers, steaks, fajitas, seafood and more. The kids' menu offers a main course, dessert, and soft drink for £8.

Lido Café. *In Hyde Park on the Serpentine Lake. South side of the Serpentine, near the Diana Princess of Wales Memorial Fountain.*

This pleasant cafeteria offers copious servings of hot meals, such as fish and chips or bangers and mash. You can also choose from fresh salads or sandwiches on whole-grain breads. There are kids' portions with sausages and chips (French fries) or chicken nuggets. Cakes and ice cream are also available. The prices are quite reasonable, especially by London standards, and there's a good view of the Serpentine Lake.

The Serpentine Bar and Kitchen. *Eastern side of the Serpentine. In Hyde Park.*

The Serpentine Bar and Kitchen serves a wide variety of tasty hot meals and snacks, freshly prepared sandwiches and salads, a daily selection of cakes and puddings from the bakery, and hot and cold drinks from the bar.

The Honest Sausage. *Kensington Gardens. In the Broad Walk, southern end, adjacent to Palace Gate.*

This eatery has two locations, one here and the other in Regent's Park. You can sample a variety of sausage dishes, hot entrees, sandwiches, and salads. Everything is organic, the meat is free-range, and in spite of the name, some of the choices are vegetarian.

Spaghetti House. *77 Knightsbridge. SW1. Tube: Hyde Park Corner.*

This restaurant is family-friendly and affordable – a welcome sight in this expensive neighborhood. There are plenty of pizzas and Italian specialties to choose from. Kids can pick a pizza or pasta along with a drink and ice cream from the children's menu. There are also several reasonably priced adult menus, which include wine or a soft drink.

Chicago Rib Shack. *145 Knightsbridge, London SW1. Tube: Hyde Park Corner.*

This restaurant serves up classic American fare, such as BBQ ribs, meatloaf, coleslaw, potato skins, spicy sweetpotato wedges, and burgers. The music is classically American as well, ranging from blues to rock and roll. All of the meat is fromfree range farms and the smoked meats are dry-rubbed with a 25 year old spice blend. The service is very kid friendly, with special treats such as face painting or animal balloons.

Noura Brasserie and Grill. *16 Hobart Place, Belgravia. London SW1. Tube: Hyde Park Corner.*

This place offers both take-out and restaurant service featuring a wide variety of Lebanese specialties. There are plenty of hot and cold appetizers, including many vegetarian choices. Main courses offer baked and skewered selections featuring lamb, chicken, quail, fish, or vegetarian options.

Spaghetti House. *47 Bryanston Street, London W1H. Tube: Marble Arch.*

Always a safe bet with kids, this restaurant offers pizza, pasta, and warm welcomes. You can also opt for salads, bruschetta, Panini, fish, or steak, and the desserts are home made. The same warm Italian welcome is extended to diners entertaining at lunch as to those out with friends of an evening. Close to Marble Arch £15-20

Harrods Department Store Food Hall. *Ground floor. 87-135 Brompton Road. SW1. Tube: Knightsbridge. Open Mon-Sat, 10-7.*

This Food Hall is filled with gourmet selections of all types, including prepared foods that you can eat in or take away. There's a rotisserie, cheese

 shop, oyster bar, sea grill, pizzeria, "Famous Deli", sushi bar, and plenty of desserts. Harrods also has a wide range of restaurants and cafés on just about every floor – ranging from an American-style diner to a French creperie, Thai place, Bagel Factory, Tapas bar, Starbucks, and a family-oriented place called Planet Harrods that shows kiddie movies on a big screen. Note: it's luxury shopping and that's reflected in the prices.

Patisserie Valerie. *215 Brompton Road. SW3. Tube: Knightsbridge or South Kensington.*

This is a good chain that offers both pastries and café meals at affordable prices. It's a great place to get a tasty meal of bangers and mash, burger, salad, or sandwich or to stop for a filling snack. The price is right and atmosphere is friendly.

Greenfield's Sandwich Emporium and Café. *12 Exhibition Road, SW7. Tube: South Kensington. Open daily.*

This pleasant café and sandwich shop is located just down Exhibition Road from the Natural History, Science, and V&A Museums. It offers a wide range of hot and cold sandwiches (even peanut butter and jelly). There are also salads and hot entrees, as well as cakes and pastries. The prices are reasonable and the food is fresh making this a very popular spot with the local lunch crowd. You can eat in or take out.

EARL'S COURT

Base2Stay. *25 Courtfield Gardens, SW5, Tube: Earl's Court. Tel. 020 7244 2255 or +44 845 262 8000; USA & Canada, call toll free: 800-511-9821. Rooms range from singles to suites, with rates £95-240 www.base2stay.com.*

This hotel is situated in a townhouse and offers a kitchenette and air conditioning in each room. It is well suited for families, offering suites, connecting rooms, and rooms with bunk beds. The décor is modern, and the hotel takes pride in being environmentally friendly. Staff is very helpful. Rooms are stocked with fair-trade tea and coffee. There are places nearby where you can buy food, and it's an easy walk to the Earl's Court tube station. An excellent find in a very handy location.

Emperor's Gate Apartment/Hotel. *Two locations: 8 Knaresborough Place and also 5 Emperor's Gate, SW5. Tel. 020 7244 8409. E-mail: info@apartment-hotels.com Tube: Earl's Court or Gloucester Road. Rates: £170 and up for 3-4 people. www.apartment-hotels.com*

These hotels are cozy and were set up by owners, who were raising three children of their own. The 1-bedroom suites can comfortably accommodate a family of 4 or 5 – one of them even has a balcony. They will supply a free crib and high chair. There is a small but well equipped kitchen and enough grocery, bakery, and take-out places nearby to make mealtimes easier and more affordable. Hotel amenities include coin-operated washer and dryer, free internet access, and free morning papers. Apartments include towels and linens, TV, private phone line, iron, and kitchen facilities. The location is very convenient to central London sights as well as direct subway access to Heathrow Airport.

Abcone Hotel. *10 Ashburn Gardens, SW7. Tel. 020 7460 3400. Tube: Gloucester Road. Rates start at £85-£99 for triple/family room. www.abcone.co.uk.*

This hotel offers clean spacious rooms and a hearty welcome. The rooms are equipped with hairdryers, TV, radio, direct-dial phone, and in-house movies. There is a free continental breakfast (a full English breakfast is available for an extra charge) and free internet access.

Travel InnHotel – London Kensington. *11 Knaresborough Place, SW5. Tel. 0870 238 3304. Tube: Earl's Court. Rates: £76 (Mon-Thurs) and £70 (Fri-Sun).*

This is a modern, budget hotel that offers good value for money. Family rooms can accommodate 2 adults and 2 kids. Breakfast is free for kids under 12.

Masala Indian Restaurant. *4 Hogarth Road, SW5. Tube: Earl's Court.*

This small restaurant has delicious Indian dishes that you can eat in or take away. Kids like it because they can see all the food ahead of time. Prices are quite reasonable, £4-£6 per dish.

Baker's Oven. *Earl's Court Road, across from the Earl's Court Tube station. SW5.*

This bakery serves lots of fresh breakfast offerings, as well as sandwiches and take-away salads for lunch or dinner.

CHELSEA

The Stockpot. *273 Kings Road. Chelsea SW3. Tube: Sloane Square.*

This restaurant is very popular with locals because the food is good and the price is right. An English breakfast is served until 6pm. You can also get pasta, salads, omelets, and specials. A 2-course lunch will cost you £5.50 and 2-course dinner is £8. There are several other Stockpot restaurants at Leicester Square, on James Street near Bond Street, and at Piccadilly Circus.

Bluebird Market and Café. *350 Kings Road. Chelsea, SW3. Tube: Sloane Square*

This market/café offers a wide choice of fresh deli foods, sandwiches, soups, and gourmet dishes. There are both indoor and outdoor tables from which to watch the activity along lively Kings Road.

Blue Kangaroo. *555 King's Road, Chelsea, and SW6. Tel. Tube: Fulham Broadway.*

This restaurant is specifically designed for families with young children. There's a soft play zone downstairs where they can romp. A large, plasma TV showing live footage of the lower level lets you keep an eye on your children, while enjoying some food –even a glass of wine or champagne. The adult menu offers a selection of fresh salads and hot dishes of risotto, salmon, chicken, pasta, fish and chips, and the like. There is an extensive kids menu. The restaurant features regular, morning entertainment for children, such as face painting and storytelling, along with special themed events, such as a Halloween Disco Party for 3-7 year olds. Another kid friendly feature: the entire place is non-smoking.

My Old Dutch Pancake House. *221 Kings Road, Chelsea, SW3. Tube: Sloane Square.*

This place not only serves up pancakes for breakfast but also offers them for lunch topped with salmon, chicken, ham, or cheese in a variety of sauces and settings. There are salads, omelets, and full English breakfasts, too.

BLOOMSBURY & THE BRITISH MUSEUM

Novotel London-St Pancras. *100-110 Euston Road, London, NW1. Tube: Kings Cross or Euston Station. Tel. 020 7666 9000 Rates start at £79. www.novotel.com/gb/hotel-5309-novotel-london-st-pancras/index.shtml*

Like all Novotels, this one is clean and contemporary and offers family deals. Your child stays for free in the parent's room along with a free buffet breakfast). There is a play area for kids in the lobby. The rooms are relatively large and comfortable, but ask for one away from Euston Road if you are a light sleeper. The hotel is located next to the British Library, near Kings Cross Station. You get the standard Novotel facilities such as air conditioning, flat screen TV, MP3 player connection, high-speed internet, iron/ironing board, hair dryer, with complimentary tea and coffee. The hotel has a fitness center, sauna, and steam room.

Crescent Hotel. *49/50 Cartwright Gardens, WC1. Tel. 020 7387 1515. Tube: Eustons, Kings Cross, or Russell Square. Rates for family rooms start at £133. www.crescenthoteloflondon.com.*

This small hotel overlooks garden across from the residence halls of the University of London. You can get keys to the gardens and tennis courts from the front desk for a small fee. They'll even lend you tennis balls and rackets. You are within easy walking distance to the wonderful Coram's Field Playground and to Harry Potter's Platform 9 3/4 at Kings Cross Train Station. The hotel welcome is warm and friendly. Although the rooms are not large they are tidy, and there are several that can accommodate a family of 3 or 4.

Wagamama. *4 Streatham Street, WC1. Tube: Tottenham Court Road.*

This restaurant is part of a chain located throughout the city that features Japanese noodles and canteen-style eating. It's fun, affordable, and kid-friendly.

REGENT'S PARK

Queen Mary's Garden Café. *In Regent's Park, near the Open-Air Theatre.*

This place, located near Queen Mary's rose garden, serves affordable, cafeteria-style food to hungry families. There is a large outdoor terrace and plenty of seats indoors, as well. You can pick a meal from a selection of hot dishes such as salmon, sausages, or pasta. You can also opt for a sandwich or go to the salad bar. There's also ice cream and pastries for an afternoon snack.

The Honest Sausage.*In Regent's Park, not too far from the London Zoo.*

This place serves free-range sausages and "Park Porkers" (a sort of hotdog), as well as soups, salads, and sandwiches – even vegetarian choices. The prices are very reasonable: ranging from £3-5 for main courses. There are tables both inside and out, where you can enjoy a meal or snack on cakes and buns.

Cow and Coffee Bean.*In Regent's Park, along Broad Walk.*

This is a great place to stop (*photo below*) if you need to refuel after a

visit to the zoo, tour of Madame Tussauds, or romp through the park. There are pastries and lots of frozen-dessert specialties, such as floats and milkshakes.

Indian YMCA Cafeteria. *41 Fitzroy Square, just south and east of Regent's Park. W1. Tel. 020 7387 0411. Tube: Warren Street.*

This place is very simple and basic. It is filled with students and regulars who appreciate traditional Indian food at bargain prices. For lunch and dinner you can choose from meat-based and vegetarian dishes. They also serve breakfast.

PADDINGTON

Thistle – Lancaster Gate Hotel. *90-92 Lancaster Gate. At corner of Bayswater Road (facing Hyde Park), W2. Tube: Queensway or Lancaster Gate. Tel. 020 845 305 8322/ (0)871 376 9022. Rates start at £145 family room.*

This large hotel is part of the Thistle chain. It is clean, modern, and attractive. The hotel has its own garden and is just across the street from Hyde Park and Kensington Gardens. It's a great location for families, including easy tube and bus access into central city sights. The rooms are not huge, but are comfortable, air-conditioned, and tastefully decorated. They come with internet access, hair dryer, iron, TV, and telephone.

Family rooms have a double bed, sofa bed, and can add a rollaway bed. The hotel offers a special kids pack and kid's menus with organic foods.

Comfort Inn – Hyde Park. *18-19 Craven Hill Gardens, W2. Tel. 020 7262 6644. Tube: Paddington. Rates start at £135.*

This is a clean, comfortable hotel on a very pretty street, west of Paddington Station. The rooms are not large, but there are triples, one quadruple, and a 2-bed apartment that can sleep 4-6 people. Two floors are reserved for non-smoking rooms.

Best Western – Paddington Court. *27 Devonshire Terrace, W2. Tel. 020 7745 1200. Rates start at £150. www.paddingtoncourt.com.*

This is a pleasant hotel on a lovely street filled with shops and cafés. It is very conveniently located near Paddington Station, Hyde Park, and Kensington Gardens. The rooms have nice amenities, including a bowl of apples, an iron, tea/coffee service, internet access, TV, and alarm clock. They vary in size, so be sure to ask for the largest one they can offer. The suites come equipped with a kitchenette featuring a microwave, sink, and fridge.

Ashley Hotel. *15-17 Norfolk Square, W2. Tel. 020 7723 3375. Tube: Paddington. Rates start at £90 for a family room. www.ashleyhotellondon.com.*

This hotel is only a block from Paddington Station on a pretty, tree-lined square. It is in a neighborhood full of bed and breakfasts – some of which are downright seedy. This one is friendly and tidy, though somewhat basic. The owner will gladly give you advice on getting around, finding places to eat, and what to do. The rooms are smallish, but clean. Some have bunk beds that fold up against the wall (like on a ship) and one queen size bed. The larger family rooms are on the lower level. A full English breakfast with cereal, juice, eggs, toast, and ham is included in the room rate. Note: there is no elevator, so you will need to carry your own luggage up and down the stairs.

NOTTING HILL

The Gate Hotel *6 Portobello Road, W11. Tel. 020 7221 0707. Tube: Notting Hill Gate. Rates: £115-135 for triple/family room. www.gatehotel.co.uk.*

This is a very pretty and friendly hotel. It is small and intimate, and ideally located for visiting Notting Hill. It is situated just at the beginning of Portobello Road, famous for its charming outdoor market. The rooms are not large, but they are bright and come equipped with a TV, minibar, and phone. A free continental breakfast is served in the room. Since there are only 7 rooms in all, it's a good idea to reserve well in advance. Special rates will be given to families booking two rooms.

Lazy Daisy Café. *59A Portobello Road. W1. Tube: Notting Hill Gate.*

This restaurant has a big, cheerful room and an outdoor terrace. It gets crowded on Saturdays when shoppers come browse through the Portobello Road street market. The café serves breakfast and lunch with offerings such as pasta, soups, panini sandwiches, baked potatoes with toppings, quiches, and salads. There is a special kids' menu or kids can ask for a half portion of the regular selections. Note: This is a non-smoking restaurant.

Manzara. *24 Pembridge Road. W11. Tube: Notting Hill Gate.*

This restaurant offers Turkish specialties to take out or eat in. These include kebabs, fish dishes, casseroles, pizzas, meat pies, and pides (meat or vegetable-filled pastries). You can also choose from a selection of big English breakfasts. The service is friendly and prices affordable.

Geales Restaurant. *2 Farmer Street. W8. Tube: Notting Hill Gate. www.geales.com.*

This is a very popular spot for traditional fish and chips. You can choose from a variety of fish: cod, plaice, salmon, or haddock. There's also the classic side dish of mushy peas. There are a few other selections on the menu, but if you don't like fish you'll be disappointed. If you do like fish (or like one of our kids, only eat fish when it's disguised under a nice crispy batter), you'll appreciate the quality, portion sizes, and reasonable prices.

Malabar. *27 Uxbridge Street. W8. Tube: Notting Hill.*

This Indian restaurant is off in a small back street and is a favorite with locals. It offers a wide range of Indian foods, with a Sunday buffet lunch where kids eat free.

EAST END

Spitalfield's Market. *Brushfield Street, E1. Tube: Liverpool Street or Algate East*

This market hall is filled with eateries, offering a variety that includes such choices as beef curry, stuffed baked potato, Thai noodles, falafel, French crepes, Mexican or Hawaiian dishes, pizza, spring rolls, Malaysian foods, and Arkansas BBQ. There's even an American Diner called Fatboy's that was originally located in Worcester, Massachusetts, then dismantled and reinstalled here.

S & M Café. *48 Brushfield Street, E1. (Across from Spitalfields Market) Tube: Liverpool Street or Algate East. www.sandmcafe.co.uk.*

The letters S and M stand for sausages and mash, which is one of the traditional British foods of-

fered here. You can also get other comfort foods, such as shepherd's pie, steak and kidney pie, fish cakes, and Toulouse sausage casserole. Side orders include some of our favorites, such as mushy pea, minted peas, and baked beans. You can select from a variety of gravies to put on your mashed potatoes. There are also salads, breakfast offerings, and a kids menu. For dessert you can choose from classics such as fruit crumble, chocolate pudding, Gooseberry Fool, and Spotted Dick. All of these are offered at very reasonable prices.

TOWER OF LONDON

Novotel London Tower Bridge. *10 Pepys Street, London EC3N. Tube: Tower Hill. Tel. 020 7265 6000. Rates start at £114. www.novotel.com/ gb/hotel-3107-novotel-london-tower-bridge/index.shtml.*

This hotel gets positive reviews from families. It is conveniently located for visits to the Tower of London, Tower Bridge, and St. Paul's Cathedral. It offers spacious family-friendly rooms with a special package, where 2 kids under 16 stay free sleeping in their parents' room (their buffet breakfast is free, too). Ask for rooms on Pepys Street if you are a light sleeper. You get the standard modern amenities of this chain; air condition-ing, flat screen TV, MP3 player connection, high-speed internet, iron/ ironing board, hair dryer, with complimentary tea and coffee. The hotel has a fitness center, sauna, and hammam (Turkish bath).

SOUTH BANK

Premier Inn. *London County Hall, Belvedere Road, London, SE1. Tube: Waterloo Station train station. Tel: 0871 527/ 0870 2383300. Rates start at £99 per night, but check for special offers. www.premierinn.com/en/hotel/LONCOU/london-county-hall.*

This hotel, located in the historic County Hall building right beside the London Eye and London Aquarium, prides itself on being family friendly. There are pull out or sofa beds for the kids and special family rates, with kids-under 16 staying for free. The restaurant has a kids menu and kids get a free breakfast for each paying adult. There are also free kid activity packs with books, activity sheets, and colored pencils. Rooms are clean and spacious. Westminster Abbey and Big Ben are just across the river.

Dolphin House. *Dolphin Square, London SW1V. Tel: +44 (0) 20 7798 8000. Tube: Pimlico or Victoria Station. Rates start at £200, but there are special deals for weekly rates. www.dolphinsquare.co.uk/house.*

 This hotel is tucked away between the Thames and Victoria Station. It is in a quiet neighborhood but still offers easy tube access to major sites. The hotel features comfortable apartments for families; ranging from studies to a 3 bedroom with 3 bathrooms. There are comfy beds, cushy bedding and towels, and fancy dishware. You can request a washing machine. There is a pool, gym, sauna, steam room, and the complex includes croquet, squash, tennis, and small shops. To be noted nearby is the Young England Kindergarten, where Princess Diana worked before marrying Prince Charles.

Novotel Waterloo. *113 Lambeth RoadSE1. Tube: Lambeth. Tel. 020 7793 1010. Rates start at £125. www.novotel.com/gb/hotel-1785-novotel-london-waterloo/index.shtml.*

The Novotel chain offers family-friendly rooms designed for 2 adults and 2 children. Up to 2 kids under 16 get free breakfast and stay in their parents' room free of charge. Tea and coffee are provided in the room. There is a play area in the hotel lobby. The location is convenient to Waterloo Station, the London Eye, and Big Ben/Westminster across the river. It is modern and convenient, if lacking a bit in old-world charm.

Hays Galleria Eateries. *London Bridge City, Tooley Street, London SE1.*

This former dock has been converted into a very pleasant shopping gallery within walking distance of Tower Bridge. There are several eateries, including a Bagel Factory that offers breakfast and lunch (food rates as okay); the Café Rouge which offers sit-down service and a choice of pastas, beef and chicken dishes, soups, salads, and quiches; and the ubiquitous Starbucks. Live bands sometimes perform near the funny central sculpture. We were treated to a good jazz ensemble.

Southwark Cathedral Refectory Café. *Southwark Cathedral. London Bridge (near Thames Walk), SE1. Tube: London Bridge.*

This place is near all the activities of Southwark and the South Bank, but offers a respite from the hustle and bustle. There's even a very nice outdoor terrace where you can sit in clement weather. The café offers cafeteria-style lunches and afternoon snacks. There are soups, sandwiches, vegetarian dishes, and very tasty desserts. In the summer, weather permitting, there are outdoor BBQs for lunch on Tuesdays and Thursdays.

Pizza Pizza Express. *New Globe Walk. SE1 (on Thames Walk, near Globe Theatre). Tube: London Bridge.*

This large restaurant is part of a chain that is present throughout London. It is very family-friendly, and by London standards, quite affordable. The pizzas offer variety and quality. There is a kid's menu. You can also pick from other pasta, salads, and Italian specialties. They are open for lunch and dinner, until midnight. We found that it was just what we needed after a visit to the Globe, Tate Modern, or Tower Bridge. You can also order pizzas to take out.

E.A.T. *3 Riverside House. Bankside, SE1 (on Thames Walk, near Golden Hinde and Globe Theatre). Tel. 020 7636 8309. Tube: London Bridge*

This self-service eatery is part of a chain that you will see in numerous locations throughout the city. It offers a wide array of freshly made sandwiches, soups, wraps, and salads (£2-3 each) that you can eat in or take out. There are interesting combinations, such as feta, lentil, and rice salad; mushroom, ricotta, and spinach sandwich; or lamb and tabouleh wrap. More classic soups and sandwiches are also available. The cookies and pastries are hard to resist, too.

Borough Market. *8 Southwark Street SE1. Located behind Southwark Cathedral, under the elevated train tracks. Tube: London Bridge. Open Fri 12-6 and Sat 9-4.*

Borough Market is known for its high quality foods, including gourmet stalls that sell everything from imported wines and olives to delicious meat pies, pastries and freshly baked bread (*see photo below*). It is a fun place to pick up a breakfast, lunch, or snack. Remember though that it's only open to the general public on Fridays and Saturdays. The rest of the week it serves as an early morning wholesale market for local shops and restaurants.

PART II: PLANNING YOUR TRIP

WHAT TO BRING

When packing, try to remember that less is better. Suitcases are heavy, and there will inevitably be times when you are the one who has to lift or carry them. Also note that big bags will take up a lot of space in your London hotel or apartment room (generally quite small by American standards) and can make it harder to find a cab. Try to stick to bags that can fit in the overhead compartment of the plane.

Most children like to pack or help pack their own bags. It is exciting and empowering. Just make sure that you maintain supervision authority (and if needed, veto power). Once they are done, go through a checklist together to ensure they haven't forgotten anything important. For London, you will want clothes that you can layer, including light fleece and rainwear. Also check for hoards of unnecessary items, or you may end up with a bag filled with stuffed animals and little else.

If your trip includes airplane travel, bring along a warm top, as transatlantic flights can be quite chilly. If you do check your bags, be sure to have essential toiletries and medicine, and emergency clothing (such as a fresh shirt, pair of socks, and underwear), luggage to last you an extra day. This will see you through if your plane or luggage is delayed. If you are traveling with a baby or small children pack several sets of clothes, snacks, small toys, and a 2-day supply of diapers and wipes in your carry-on luggage to get through the flight and first day.

If friends or family members are looking for good travel gifts for your kids' trip, you might want to suggest:
- Kid-friendly cameras
- Easy-to-pack art supplies
- Travel-sized toys, games, or activity books
- Small day-packs, small roller-board suitcases
- Toiletries' kit filled with travel-sized toothbrush, toothpaste, shampoo, comb, brush, etc
- Walky-talkies
- Binoculars
- Travel diary or notebook
- iPod
- Kindle or recorded books, preferably with some favorite titles featuring London or English characters
- Deck of cards or travel-size versions of favorite games

WHAT TO KNOW BEFORE YOU GO

Passports: Each member of your family must have a valid passport to enter Britain. No visa is necessary for stays of less than three months. If you need to obtain or renew a passport for any member of your family, do not put it off until the last minute. It can take as many as 90 days to process – even longer if you need to obtain a copy of your birth certificate or other required proofs of citizenship or identity. Passport application forms and instructions are available at your local Passport Agency Office, county courthouse, some post offices, and some travel agencies. They are also accessible online at: *travel.state.gov/passport_services.html* or you can get them via mail by calling the National Passport Information Center, *Tel. 900/225-5674.*

Be aware that as of July 2, 2001, any child under the age of 14 must have an application signed by BOTH parents, or submit proof that a sole parent has custody or guardianship of that child. Remember, too, that although adult passports are valid for 10 years, children's passports are only valid for 5 years.

Climate: London is more famous for rain and fog than it is for clear, blue skies. That said, the climate of London is actually relatively mild. Summer temperatures generally hover between 60 and 80 degrees Fahrenheit. In the winter, even though London is well north of any U.S. city (except in Alaska) and roughly on the same latitude as Winnipeg, Manitoba, the temperature rarely drops below freezing and snow is a rare sight. One thing that you can count on in London is frequent changes in the weather, even during the course of one day. As a result, you'll want to dress in layers, even in the summer, and be prepared to put them on and peel them off repeatedly. Winters can be damp, so bring a sweater or fleece to ward off the cold. You might want to bring a folding umbrella and pack a rain jacket for each member of your family (lightweight ones are fine in the summer). If you want to hear the latest weather forecast while you're in London: *Tel. 0906 654 3268, 60p per minute.*

Health insurance: Before you leave home, contact your health insurance company to see if it covers medical expenses abroad. If so, don't forget to bring along your membership card. If not, you may want to purchase supplemental health insurance for travelers. Here are some options:

Several companies sell travel health insurance. The website www.insuremytrip.com allows you to compare plans. The US Department of State maintains an extensive list of providers at: *travel.state.gov/ medical.html.*

Note: **If you are a teacher or university faculty member** you can take advantage of the free health and accident coverage that comes with the purchase of an international teacher's ID card. International youth and student cards also offer coverage for children and students ages 12 to 26 years. Either card costs $22. Each one covers hospital stays, medical expenses, emergency evacuation, accidental death and dismemberment, repatriation of remains, passport protection, and baggage delay insurance. The ID also gives you discounts for entry to museums, monuments, and shows. Contact: **Council Travel**, *Tel. 800/2COUNCIL*, or your local Council Travel Office (often located in or near universities).

LONDON-THEMED BOOKS FOR KIDS
Fiction

A Bear Called Paddington, and other Paddington stories, by Michael Bond. These are the adventures of a small, stuffed bear lost in Paddington Train Station with a sign around his neck reading "Please look after this bear. Thank You." He is adopted by a family and discovers a new life in London.

Madeline in London, by Ludwig Bemelmans. The girls who live in two straight lines visit their friend Pepito in London. There are lovely illustrations of London sights.

William Shakespeare & the Globe, by Aliki. An introduction to the playwright and his theater filled with the usual poetry and charm of Aliki's illustrations along with quotes from the Bard.

Peter Pan, by JM Barrie. A story about the boy who never wants to grow up and takes Londoners Jane, John, and Michael on a big adventure filled with pirates, mermaids, Indians, and a tiny fairy. It's the tale that served as inspiration for the wonderful Princess Diana Memorial Playground in Kensington Gardens.

When We Were Very Young, by A.A. Milne. This collection of delightful children's poems features Christopher Robin and includes charming London moments such as "At the Zoo" and "Changing of the Guard."

The Lion, the Witch, and the Wardrobe (and other books in the Chronicles of Narnia series) by C.S. Lewis. Four children discover a magic door in a London closet that takes them to a new world of adventures.

Harry Potter books, by J.K. Rowling. Although most of the adventures of this young wizard take place at Hogwarts School of Witchcraft and Wizardry somewhere in the English countryside, there are scenes that take place in the London Zoo, at King's Cross Train Station, aboard a triple-decker bus, and in the neat rows of suburban houses that you see from the trains to and from Heathrow Airport.

The Shakespeare Stealer and **Shakespeare's Scribe**, by Gary Blackwood. Two books that describe the adventures of a young orphan boy who joins Shakespeare's troupe of London players in the early 1600s.

King of Shadows, by Susan Cooper. This book is also set in Elizabethan London and involves a modern boy transported back in time to Shakespeare's Globe Theatre.

Petals in the Ashes, by Mary Hooper. A story of two sisters who live through the Great Fire of London in 1666.

The Ravenmaster's Secret: Escape from the Tower of London, by Elvira Woodruff. An 11-year old boy takes care of the Tower ravens and ends up helping to organize a prisoners' escape.

Oliver Twist, A Christmas Carol, and other classics by Charles Dickens. A portrayal of poverty and social inequities in Victorian London.

Around the World in 80 Days, by Jules Verne (look for the kid-friendly Eyewitness Classics version from Dorling Kindersley publishers). Phineas Fogg's great race begins in Victorian London.

Dracula, by Bram Stoker (look for the kid-friendly Eyewitness Classics version from Dorling Kindersley publishers). While most of the action takes place in Transylvania, there are scenes that take place in London and other parts of England. Author Stoker wrote the book while he was living in London's Chelsea neighborhood.

Pride and Prejudice, Sense and Sensibility, and other classics by Jane Austen. Although only a few scenes take place in London, they provide an interesting portrait of early 19th century England and are a great read, besides.

Child-friendly versions of Shakespeare's plays. There are many options, from graphic novels to simplified stories and animated renditions.

Non-Fiction

This is London, by M. Sasek. This picture book was written decades ago, but has recently been re-edited. It still delights with 1950s-60s era-style illustrations of London's sights and culture.

Dorling Kindersley Eyewitness Books. Several books in this series provide good background, including **Shakespeare, Viking, Pirate, Medieval Life, Castle, Knight,** and **Arms and Armor.**

London (Great Cities Through The Ages), by Neil Morris. A good, kid-friendly review of London's history from Roman times to the present.

Introduction to Art: In Association With the National Gallery, London, by Rosie Dickins, Mari Griffith, Jane Chisholm. A great resource on art for kids and adults.

Horrible Histories published by Hippo. A wonderful series that teaches kids how history can be fun. Ones relevant to London's history include: **The Terrible Tudors, Even More Terrible Tudors, The Slimy Stuarts, The Gorgeous Georgians, The Vile Victorians, The Blitzed Brits, The Cut-throat Celts, The Smashing Saxons, The Vicious Vikings,** and **The Stormin' Normans.**

Smelly Old History series by Mary Dobson, published by Oxford University Press. Another delightful and informative series that gives kids facts on history and makes it fun. There are even scratch and sniff sections to highlight the odorous English past. Examples in the series include: **Medieval Muck, Tudor Odours, Reeking Royals,** and **Victorian Vapours.**

LONDON-THEMED FILMS FOR KIDS

The 101 Dalmations, the version with real actors has scenes filmed in St. James Park

Mary Poppins, full of magic and memorable images of London

The Great Mouse Detective, a clever cartoon story, based on the Sherlock Holmes character.

The Swan Princess, the theme of a swan princess is used for kids' programs at Leeds Castle, famous for its swans and other birds.

What a Girl Wants, set in contemporary London, an American girl gets to know London and a long lost father

Agent Cody Banks 2: Destination London. Cool spy Cody Banks has to go undercover in London to save the world's leaders from falling under the spell of a diabolical villain.

Chronicles of Narnia, The Lion, the Witch, and the Wardrobe and Prince Caspian. Though not much of these tales takes place in London, they tell the magical adventures of Pevenses children originally sent away from London to the country to get away from the Blitz during WWII.

The **Harry Potter** movies, based on the world-famous series of 7 books, chronicling the adventures of a young wizard, his friends and teachers, and the evil forces they must combat that threaten their world.

Oliver Twist, a Dickens classic set among poor street urchins of 19th century London.

My Fair Lady, another classic featuring the story of Eliza Dolittle, a flower-selling Cockney-accented who is transformed into a lady.

Notting Hill, a romance that may appeal to teens, set in London with Hugh Grant and Julia Roberts.

The World is Not Enough, a James Bond movie that uses London as the backdrop for its opening scenes.

Shakespeare in Love, a romance, also for teens, filled with scenes from Romeo and Juliette.

A Lion in Winter, though none of it takes place in London, it's a great introduction to the history of Henry II, Eleanor of Aquitaine, Richard the Lionheart, and King John.

King Arthur (the recent one), again it doesn't take place in London and is based on a legend, but gives a good idea of early Celtic tribes, the Saxon Invaders, and the Roman occupiers of England.

Return to Neverland, a fictionalized story based on the real author J.M. Barrie, who lived near Kensington Gardens, where he found the inspiration for his Peter Pan tales.

GETTING TO LONDON
Flying

Generally speaking, you will save money on airfares if you book your tickets 4-6 months in advance, especially for travel during the summer or Christmas Holiday. If you can travel to London during Spring Break, Thanksgiving, or other off-season times of the year, you will find much lower travel fares than during the summer. However, discounts and charter tickets vary greatly from year to year, so there is no hard, fast rule. Keep your eye out for special fares advertised in major newspapers or on line. Airlines often advertise special deals, sometimes with a free night or two of hotel thrown in to boot. Remember to ask about reduced fares for children. If you have a trusted travel agent, this is a good place to start looking for bargain airfares.

You can also let your fingers do the walking online at sites such as **Expedia** (*www.expedia.com*); **Travelocity** (*www.travelocity.com*); and **Orbitz** (*www.orbitz.com*), which allow you to compare flights and rates on several major airlines. You can also surf the web for travel consolidators with names such as cheaptickets.com or budgettravel.com that can easily save you 25% on flights and car rentals. Several car rental consolidators such as **AutoEurope** (*Tel. 888/223-5555; www.autoeurope.com*) and **Kemwel** (*Tel. 877/820-0668; www.kemwel.com*) also sell discounted flights. Another option is European airlines such as Virgin Atlantic or Aer Lingus (see below for contact information) for lower fares.

Note that rules vary from one airline to another regarding children's discounts, how to seat babies, and regulations about traveling with young children. Check for specifics with your travel agent or directly with the airline.

Here are some tips for planning your plane trip:

• While most transatlantic trips towards Europe are overnight flights, some airlines (e.g. British Air and American Airlines) offer daytime flights to London from Boston or New York. These may be a less stressful alternative to spending the night on board an airplane with small children.

• If you do take the overnight transatlantic flight, try to book it as late in the evening as possible. The later you leave, the more likely you (and your kids) will get some sleep. Also, the later you arrive in London, the more likely your body clock will be ready to face a new day.

• Bring your own food. Pack snacks or pick up some take-out food at the airport, though beware that you will not be able to carry beverages or liquids through security. This way you can eat what you like, when you want, and throw it away before you land.

• The return flight from London to the US is always a daytime trip. Be sure to bring plenty of small toys, (diapers, if needed), books, snacks, activities, and entertainment.

• Take advantage of stopovers and connections. Let kids stretch their legs, get some food, and watch other planes take off and land. If you are facing a long layover in an interesting city, consider extending it even more so that you can leave the airport and see some sights.

Here are some of the major carriers offering flights from the US to London, as of December 2009. However, note that some US airlines are facing bankruptcies or consolidations, so check the financial health of an airline before you book:

- **British Airways** – *Tel. 800/247-9297; www.britishairways.com*
- **Aer Lingus** (connections through Ireland) – *Tel. 800/IRISH AIR (800/ 474 7424); www.aerlingus.com*
- **Virgin Atlantic** – *Tel. 203-750-2000; www.virginatlantic.com*
- **American Airlines** – *Tel. 800/433-7300; www.aa.com*
- **Continental Airlines** – *Tel. 800/231-0856; www.continental.com*
- **Delta Airlines** – *Tel. 800/241-4141; www.delta.com*
- **Northwest Airlines** – *Tel. 800/447-4747; www.nwa.com*
- **United Airlines** – *Tel. 800/241-6522; www.united.com*
- **USAIR** – *Tel. 800/622-1015; www.ual.com*

GETTING TO & FROM THE AIRPORTS
Heathrow Airport

Heathrow is located 24 kilometers (15 miles) west of London. It is well linked to the city via public transportation. There are multiple options:

Heathrow Express Train (*www.heathrowexpress.com*). Quick and easy, but more expensive than some alternatives. Located directly in the

airport, it gets you into Paddington Station (central London) in 15 minutes. Daily trains run every 15 minutes between 5 am and midnight. Economy fare tickets are £16.50 for a one-way adult fare, £32 for round trip, and half price for kids under age 16. From Paddington Station you can connect to points all over the city through the London subway (called the Tube or Underground). You can purchase the whole ticket for the ride into London and on the subway at Heathrow. They sometimes offer summer promotions where kids travel free.

Piccadilly Line Tube train. Regular subway (Tube) service, less rapid than Heathrow Express, but also cheaper (£4) and may be more convenient if you are heading to spots on this route, such as Earl's Court, South Kensington, Knightsbridge, Hyde Park Corner, Piccadilly Circus, Covent Garden, Bloomsbury, or Kings Cross Train Station. The subway station is right in the airport.

National Express Coach Company. Bus service that links Heathrow to Victoria Train Station in London. Buses depart from Heathrow Central Bus Station between Terminals 1, 2, and 3 every 30 minutes and the journey takes about 45 minutes (longer during rush hour). One-way fare is £5.

Dot 2 Dot hotel shuttles. Shared hotel shuttle buses to any hotel in the city. Cost: £17 per person.

London Taxi. These are spacious and comfortable but very expensive (£50-70) and may take far longer than the trains if there is a lot of traffic.

Note: The Heathrow lost and found phone number is: *8745 7727*.

Gatwick Airport

This airport is located 50 kilometers (30 miles) south of London. Unless you have bundles of money and time, do not try to take a taxi. The ride will take over an hour and the bill will be £100 or more. Public transit options include:

Gatwick Express Train, which runs every quarter hour and connects the airport to Victoria Train Station in central London in about 30 minutes. One-way fares are £16.90 for adults and half price for kids. **First Capital Trains** go from Gatwick to London Bridge station and to several stops through London to Kings Cross. Fare is £8.90 for adults. **Southern Trains** run the same route as the Gatwick Express, but make more stops. The cost is lower: £10.90 per adult.

The Gatwick Airport lost and found phone number is: *01 293 503162*.

TRAIN STATIONS

If you arrive in London via the **Eurostar** train from France or Belgium you will arrive at London's St Pancras Station. Kings Cross and St. Pancras International Stations stand adjacent to one another and share the same Underground Station. If you are planning on leaving London on the Eurostar train, note that you will save a lot of money by booking your tickets in advance, online at www.eurostar.com or through many U.S.-based travel companies and sites. There are reduced rates for kids and youths. All fares vary considerably depending on your travel dates and how far in advance you book.

Information on other trains and fares in and out of London are available at: http://www.nationalrail.co.uk/

Major London train stations include:

Charing Cross Station: Services Kent, Hastings, and SE London

Elephant and Castle Station: Trains to southern London suburbs

Euston Station: Services Birmingham, Manchester, and overnight trains to Glasgow

King's Cross Station: Services NE towns, such as Cambridge, York, Durham, Newcastle, and Glasgow or Edinburgh, Scotland. Also trains to Hogwarts School of Witchcraft and Wizardry.

Paddington Station: Express train to Heathrow Airport. Services W England and S Wales including towns such as Windsor, Oxford, and Reading.

St. Pancras Station: Eurostar trains. Also services East Midlands and Yorkshire regions of England.

Victoria Station: Express trains for Gatwick Airport. Service to Leeds and other towns in the regions of Kent, Surrey, and Sussex.

Waterloo: Service to SE England, including Kent, Surry, and Sussex. Trains to Windsor/Eton.

Tourist Information Centers

There are tourist information centers at: Heathrow Airport Terminals 1, 2, 3, and the airport Tube station; Liverpool Street Tube station; Victoria Train Station Forecourt; Waterloo Train Station Arrivals Hall. Euston Rail Station opposite Platform 8. The **Britain and London Visitors Center** is located at: *1 Lower Regent Street, SW1 (Tube: Piccadilly Circus), phone: 08701 566 366*. **City of London Information Center** is at: *St. Paul's Churchyard, EC4 (Tube: St. Paul's)*. The **Southwark Information Center** is right next to London Bridge at: *#6 Tooley St, SE1*. You can get cultural information in the kiosk across from St. Paul's Cathedral (no hotel information) and in Vinopolis on the South Bank.

BASIC INFORMATION

Electricity

In Britain the electric current is set at 240 volts, compared to only 120 in the United States. This means that if you try to plug an American appliance into a British socket, you will likely blow out its engine. Note: many portable computers, as well as camera or phone rechargers can automatically handle 240 volt currents. Check your owners' manual or the information on your device.

The plugs in Britain are also a different shape than those in either the United States or continental Europe. As a result, if you want to use an American appliance in London, you will need an adapter (to fit the plug) with a transformer (to translate from 240 volts to 120). You can purchase these in travel or electrical gadget stores in the States or in airports, local chemist shop, or large department stores.

Emergencies

Dial 999 for police, fire, or ambulance services.

Also consider contacting the U.S. Embassy in London: *Grosvenor Square. Tel. 0207 499 9000.*

Health

Drug stores are called chemists', and are staffed with medically trained professionals who can give you advice regarding minor complaints. If you are really sick, ask your hotel or local chemist for the nearest hospital. This happened to a friend of ours whose daughter developed a fever and ear infection during their stay in London. They were referred to the nearest public hospital, where they waited 20 minutes to be seen, left with a diagnosis and prescription, and were told there was no charge for the visit. This was overly generous. Normally, only citizens of European Union countries are offered free care by the British National Health Care system.

Here are some useful health tips:

• Be sure to fill out the emergency contact information page in the passport of each family member.

• If you or any member of your family uses a prescription medication, bring enough to cover your trip. Ask your health care provider to give you a prescription with the generic name in case you need a refill.

• Britain uses the metric system. Know your child's weight in pounds and divide it by 2.2 to convert it to kilos. You may need to know this to find the proper dosage for medications if you need to buy some for your child while in London.

• Bring your own fever thermometer. British ones calculate temperature in Celsius not Fahrenheit.

• Here is a list of handy things to have when you travel with kids: fever-reducing/ pain relieving medication (kid and adult varieties), antihistamine/ decongestant such as Benadryl, anti-itch cream, antibiotic first aid cream, Band-Aids, tweezers, a fever thermometer, tablets for indigestion, eye drops, and a sewing kit (needle, thread, safety pins).

Holidays & Business Hours

Most shops and museums are open daily, 10-6 or so. Many have stay open later on Thursdays. Major department stores are generally closed on Sundays but stay open late on Thursdays.

Public holidays in Britain include: 1 January-New Years Day; Good Friday-Friday before Easter; Easter Sunday and Easter Monday; May Day-

1st Monday in May; Bank Holiday-Last Monday in May; Bank Holiday-Last Monday in August; Christmas-December 25; Boxing Day-December 26.

Language Differences

"The Americans are identical to the British in all respects except, of course, language." – *Oscar Wilde*

One of the pleasures of traveling to Britain as an American is to discover the similarities and differences in our common language of English. Overall, it's easy to get around and understand what's going on, but there really are many differences, especially in the use of slang and common terms. Here are some examples:

• A game of arrows is a game of darts.
• Bangers and mash is a plate of sausages and mashed potatoes.
• A biscuit is a cookie and a scone is a biscuit.
• A bitter is beer, served in pint and half-pint measures.
• A bloke is a man.
• A Bobby is a police officer.
• The bonnet is the hood of a car.
• The boot is the trunk of a car.
• A call box is a phone booth.
• A chemist's is a drug store.
• Chips are French fries.
• The City, is a central area of London, containing the financial district
• Crisps are potato chips.
• A coach is a tour bus.
• A cuppa is a cup of tea.
• A digestive biscuit is a cookie.
• A dressing gown is a bathrobe.
• The Eye or London Eye is a giant Ferris wheel.
• A fancy dress party is a costume party.
• The first floor is one flight up (what Americans would consider the second floor).
• A flat is an apartment, not a punctured tire (spelled tyre in England).
• Football is soccer.
• Footpath is a sidewalk.
• The gents is the men's room.
• A hoover is a vacuum cleaner and hoovering means you are vacuuming.
• Jelly is jello. If you want something to spread on your bread ask for jam.
• A jumper is a sweater, not a sleeveless dress.

- Kerb is the gutter.
- The ladies is the ladies' rest room.
- A lift is an elevator.
- Marmite something to spread on toast made of yeast extract.
- Nappies are diapers.
- The Orbital is the ring road highway around London – it may feel like it takes 365 days to drive all the way around.
- A Pasty or Cornish Pasty is a vegetable or meat-filled pastry.
- A pie is generally a meat pie. With fruits it's more likely to be called a tart.
- A pitch is a playing field.
- A pillar box is a mail box
- Posh is fancy or upper class
- A Public School is actually a private school in England. Publicly-funded schools are called State Schools.
- Pudding is dessert.
- A queue is a line in which you wait. To queue up is to get in line.
- A quid is one pound sterling.
- A roundabout is a traffic circle.
- A rubber is an eraser.
- Rubbish is trash and you dispose of it in a rubbish bin or dustbin.
- Rugger means rugby.
- The Season means the social season (June-August).
- To skive off means to skip work or school.
- Spotted Dick is a dessert.
- Stout is an Irish beer.
- A subway is an underpass, not the underground train station.
- Ta means thank you.
- A toad-in-the-hole is similar to an American pig-in-a-blanket.
- Tomato sauce can be ketchup.
A torch is a flashlight.
- Trousers are pants.
- The Tube and the Underground are both terms for the subway, and a Subway is a passage under a busy street.
- VAT or value added tax is a 17.5% sales tax.
- Wellingtons or Wellies are rain boots name for the Duke of Wellington.
- A Zebra Crossing is a crosswalk marked by a black and white pole, where cars are supposed to stop for pedestrians. You may remember the one on the Beatles' Abbey Lane album (*see photo on page 93*).

Laundry

While laundry can be just a menial chore at home, it can become a real challenge when you are traveling, especially with messy kids. We've encountered a variety of strategies for dealing with this issue:

• Let it pile up. One family we know packed enough cheap socks and underwear to last the whole trip and just threw them away after each use. For the rest, they packed enough to wear for three weeks. This works, but means you'll have lots of luggage and suitcases filled with dirty clothes by the end of your trip.

• Drop it off at a bulk laundry or dry cleaner – an easy but expensive option.

• Use a launderette – the British version of a Laundromat.

• Hand wash your clothes in the hotel sink. Just don't cover your room in drippy clothes – it won't go over well with your hosts. Try to dry them on hangers over the tub, sink, or window sill.

• Use the hotel laundry or dry-cleaning services. Ask at the front desk.

• Stay in a short-term apartment equipped with a washing machine.

Money Matters

Cash: Although Britain is a member of the European Union it has not adopted the Union's common currency, the Euro. Instead you will need to obtain British pounds. The easiest way to do this is to use your ATM card (or credit card with a PIN) in a cash dispensing machine much as you would at home. ATM machines are widely available, including at the airport and in train stations. This method is both convenient and the most likely to give you a decent exchange rate. If you want to change cash or traveler's checks (in pounds or foreign currency), you will be dependent on finding an open bank or exchange office and will face high transaction costs and fees.

Note: London is an expensive city, especially when it comes to food and lodging! At press time the exchange rate was about 1.60 US dollars to 1 British pound. Listed prices looked similar to those we'd see in the United States, except that they represented a cost that was more than 50% higher. As a result, we have tried to make recommendations throughout this book of ways to save money, enjoy activities that are available free of charge or for low prices, and find more reasonably priced places to eat and sleep.

Credit Cards

Both Visa and Master Card are widely accepted in hotels, restaurants, museums, shops, and tourist attractions. American Express, Discover, and Diners Club are not widely accepted. If you lose your credit card, report it to the local police and call:

•**Visa 24-hour service:** *Tel. 0 800 895 082*
•**MasterCard 24-hour service:** *Tel. 0 800 964 767*

Public Restrooms

Take advantage of public toilets in museums and other tour sights; public playgrounds; department stores; and restaurants. Many of these have baby changing stations. Occasionally, you will run across a pay toilet installed in an automated cabin on a city sidewalk.

Safety

London is a relatively safe city, especially the popular tourist and residential areas. As always, you do need to exercise common street sense.

You biggest concern will be how to **safely navigate street crossings** and traffic. This is especially tricky since the British drive on the left side of the street, so instead of looking to the left first when you are crossing a street you need to look to the right for the cars in the lane closest to you. Of course, this doesn't always count if it's a one-way street. It's very confusing for those of us used to driving on the right. Our solution was to double-check each way twice before crossing a street. Fortunately, many crosswalks in London have directions written on the pavement telling you which way to look.

Also, be mindful of **pickpockets**. As a foreign visitor you are an obvious target for modern-day Artful Dodgers. Stay alert as to the whereabouts of your wallet and valuables – especially in crowded tourist areas or on public transportation.

Our greatest fear as parents has always been that of losing track of our children in an unfamiliar place. Here are some tips to lessen the risk and anxiety of a **lost child**:

• If your children are old enough, have them learn the name of your hotel, hosts, or street and address where you are staying. Show them where it is on a map. Point out nearby landmarks. Pick up several of your hotel's business cards at the front desk and distribute one to each member of your group.

• If your children are small, secure a label to their clothes, such as the paper luggage labels you get at the airport. Include the child's name, your name, and your address and phone information in London. Make sure to show you kids what you are doing and explain why, with words such as, "If you are ever lost, this tag will show a grownup your name and where we are staying, so we can find you."

- When visiting a large museum or sight, be sure to establish an easy-to-find meeting place in case you become separated.
- Teach your children the age-old rule of staying in one place if they do get lost. You are more likely to find them if they are not a moving target. We also tell our kids to use the same advice we give at home. If you are lost, tell an official helper (like a police officer or museum guard) or look for another family with children and ask them to help.
- Don't forget to keep track of your adult companions, too. While my husband and I have yet to lose a child in a foreign place, we have lost track of each other. Be sure to have a meeting plan if you are off on separate missions, and throw in a back-up plan just in case.
- Equip everyone with a walky talky. Modern ones are lightweight, easy to use, and have a range of 2 miles or more. They come in sets of two or four. You can also buy multiple sets and set them all to the same frequency. Not only can you use these to keep track of each other, but they are also handy when you need to stand in a long line. One adult can queue up, while the rest of the group looks at souvenirs, gets a snack, or runs around until it is nearly your turn.

Sports & Recreation

Bicycling: London traffic is congested and, due to the fact that they drive on the left, very confusing. As a result, your best bet for family biking is to join a tour or stick to the large public parks and walkways along the river. The London Bicycle Tour Company at 1A Gabriel's Wharf, South Bank, (Tube: Waterloo) offers group outings and bike rentals, including kids' bikes and ride-ons. Fat Tires Bike Tours offers rides for families. The meeting point is just outside the Queensway Underground (Central Line) stop. For more information: *www.FatTireBikeToursLondon.com, Tel. +44 (0)788 233 8779.* There is also a very fun bike rental spot in Battersea Park, near the tennis courts by the path that runs parallel to the Thames. Called London Recumbents, it rents a good selection of goofy 1- and 2-person bikes for people of all ages and sizes.

Boating: You can rent rowboats and paddleboats on the Serpentine in Hyde Park or the Boating Lake in Regent's Park. Regent's Park also has a special kids' boating pond. Sailing enthusiasts will enjoy watching the model sail boat races at Hyde Park's Round Pond or the Boating Pond in Hampstead Heath. There are numerous rowing races along the Thames throughout the year, including a famous one west of London at Henley. Crew enthusiasts can also check out the River & Rowing Museum in Henley. There are hourly trains from Paddington Station.

Bowling: The Queens Ice Bowl, *17 Queensway, near NW corner of Kensington Gardens, Tube: Bayswater. (Tel. 0207 229 0172)* has ten lanes devoted to 10-pin bowling.

Horseback Riding: If you've always dreamed of riding a horse through Hyde Park here is your chance. Contact **Hyde Park Stables** at *Tel. 0207 723 2813 or Ross Nye Stables at Tel. 0207 262 3791, located on the N side of the Park.*

Ice Skating: There is an indoor rink near the *NW corner of Kensington Gardens at the Queens Ice Bowl, 17 Queensway, Tube: Bayswater.* In the winter there are outdoor rinks above the Liverpool Street Station; at **Somerset House** (*The Strand, WC2. Tube: Charing Cross*); and above the Marble Arch Tube station. Skate rentals are available.

Rollerblading: There are special lanes reserved for rollerblades and bicycles in Hyde Park (along the Serpentine) and Kensington Gardens (via Queensway Gate). You can rent rollerblades from **Queens Skate Shop**, *35 Queensway, on the NW Side of Kensington Gardens, Tel. 0207 727 4669;* or from **Slick Willies** on the S side of Kensington Gardens, *41 Kensington High Street, Tel. 0207 937 3824.* You can also rent rollerblades at Slam City Skates, *near Covent Garden at 16 Neal's Yard, Tel. 0207/240-09-28.*

Rugby: It's the sport that inspired American football. To learn more and see a match, you can visit the Museum of Rugby and go on a guided, behind-the-scenes tour of **Twickenham Stadium**, *Rugby Road, Twickenham, Greater London, TW1, Tel. 020 8892 8877.*

Running or Jogging: There are plenty of great spots along the North or South Banks of the Thames, as well as in London's beautiful public parks.

Soccer (called Football in Britain): To kick around your own soccer ball, head for the open green spaces in London's major parks. If you want to learn more about professional English soccer, you can go to Chelsea and take a full behind-the-scenes tour of the club's stadium. **Chelsea Football Club**, *Stamford Bridge, Fulham Road, SW6. Tube: Fulham Broadway, Tel. 0870 603 0005.* Although it's difficult to get tickets for matches, you can check out the possibilities on the website: www.chelseafc.com

Swimming: There is outdoor swimming at the **Serpentine Lido** in Hyde Park. It's basically a roped off section of the lake, and there's a kids

162 LONDON WITH KIDS

paddle pool. Hampstead Heath also has bathing ponds and an outdoor Lido pool. The **Central YMCA**, *112 Russell St, off Tottenham Court Road (Tel. 0207 343 1700)*, has an indoor pool.

Tennis: There are tennis courts in Hyde Park (*Tel. 020 7262 3474*), Regent's Park (*Tel. 0207 486 4216*), and Battersea Park (T*el. 0208 871 7542*). If you want to watch the pros play on grass courts or enjoy the Tennis Museum, head out to **Wimbledon**. By Tube, take the District line to Southfields, then Bus 493 to the **All England Lawn Tennis & Croquet Club**, *Church Road, Wimbledon, London SW19*. Enter through Gate 4 for Centre Court where the museum is located.

Telephones

The area code for London is 020. London phone numbers are 8-digits. If you are calling a London phone number from within the city, skip the 020 area code and just dial the 8-digit number. Use the area code if you are dialing a London number from somewhere else in the U.K.

If you are calling a London phone number from abroad, the country code for England is "44." Then dial "20" for London, followed by the 8-digit phone number.

If you want to make an international call from London, dial 00, then the country code, followed by the area code and local number. Here is a list of country codes: United States – 1; Canada – 1; Hawaii – 1808; Puerto Rico – 1809; Australia – 61; Austria – 43; Belgium – 32; France – 33; Germany – 49; Greece – 30; Hong Kong – 852; India – 91; Ireland – 353; Israel – 972; Italy – 39; Japan – 81; Mexico – 52; Netherlands – 31; New Zealand – 64; Norway – 47; Portugal – 351; Spain – 34; Sweden – 46; Switzerland – 41.

Here are some handy phone numbers within London:
- **Emergencies (fire, police, ambulance) – 999**
- International dialing code – 00
- Local and national directory enquiries – 118 500
- International directory enquiries – 153
- Local and national operator – 100
- International operator – 155
- Collect calls – 155
- Time – 123

Skype: The easiest and by most affordable way to call people in England or across the world if you have access to a computer is to use Skype. Information on downloading and using this service is available at: *www.skype.com*

Public Phones: The trademark red call boxes and other public phones in London accept coins (10p, 20p, 50p or £1), phone cards, and charge cards. You can purchase a phone card worth £3, £5, £10, or £20 from any newspaper or stationery store or at the post office. A display on the phone tells you how much money is left on your card throughout the call.

Cellular Phones: Some U.S. cell phones work on the GSM (Global Standard for Mobiles) system, but confirm this before you go, and call your provider company ahead of time to ensure they enable your international service. Count on spending $1-2 per minute for each call.

You can rent a cell phone to use in Europe from American companies such as **Intouch USA** (*Tel. 703/222-7161, www.intouchusa.com*); **TravelCell** (*Tel. 877/CELL-PHONE, www.travelcell.com*); **Cellular Abroad** (*Tel. 800/287-3020; www.cellularabroad.com*); **Rent a Cellular** (*Tel. 877/902-7368; www.rent-a-cellular.com*). Car rental companies such as **Europecar** (*Tel. 888/223-5555; www.autoeurope.com*); and **Kemwel** (*Tel. 877/820-0668; www.kemwel.com*) also rent cell phones and may offer special deals if you use them to book plane or car reservations. Plan on spending $25-$50/week for the phone rental, plus an access and shipping charge in some cases. Local and long-distance calls will run you $1-$2/minute.

Another option is to rent a cell phone while you are in London. There are several companies such as **Rent-A-Mobile** (*Tel. 01704 544015, www.rent-a-mobile.co.uk*); **Mobell** (*www.mobell.com*); or **Cellhire** (*www.cellhire.com*). Ask if you can have the phone delivered to you at the airport or your London hotel.

Time

London is 5 hours ahead of New York, 6 hours ahead of Chicago, 7 hours ahead of Denver, and 8 hours ahead of San Francisco. It is in the same time zone as Ireland and Portugal, but is 1 hour behind the time in France, Italy, Spain, Switzerland, Belgium, and Germany.

Tipping

Most restaurants will include a tip (called "service") with your bill, otherwise add 10%. This is also the rate for tipping taxi drivers and hairdressers. Expect to tip a tour guide £1-2.

Video/DVD Formats

British televisions are set to a different standard of lines per frame, called SECAM, than are American ones which function on the NTSC standard. As a result, you cannot use American-made videos in a British machine or vice versa. Similarly, DVDs are set to different standards across 6 world regions. The US and Canada are in region I and Europe is in region II. If your disc is coded to a specific region, it will not function on a disc player manufactured in a different region. However, some DVDs are not coded for any particular region and will play anywhere.

INDEX

Things Change!
Phone numbers, prices, addresses, quality of service – all change.
If you come across any new information, let us know. No item is too small!

Contact us at :

jopenroad@aol.com

or

www.openroadguides.com

PHOTO CREDITS

The following photos are from Betty Borden: p. 9; p. 79 top; p. 120; p. 121 bottom; 122; p. 130.

The following photos are from wikimedia commons: back cover and p. 61: Graeme Maclean; p. 1: aurelian; p. 7: Andrew Dunn; p. 8: Tony Hisgett; p. 43: Oxfordian Kissuth; p. 52: Xehpuk; p. 60: Garry Knight; p. 71: Panos Asproulis; p. 74: Uli Harder; p. 86: Stephen McKay; p. 97: geograph.org.uk; p. 99: Andrew Dunn; p. 100; p. 114: simdaperce; p. 134: Richard Croft.

The following images are from flickr.com: front cover photo and p. 11: alecea; p. 3 top: alexbrn; p. 3 bottom: neiljs; p. 10: Keith Roper; p. 14: Andy Hay; p. 22: mac morrison; p. 25: cvconnell; p. 28: nicksarebi; p. 29: Todd Huffman; p. 30: laszlo-photo; p. 37: mostaque; p. 38: Rev Stan; p. 41: Wolfiewolf; p. 45: Jaume Maneses; p. 46: apdk; p. 48: ahisgett; p. 49: mrdoubtfire; p. 51: Ian Muttoo; p. 55: NuriaMT; p. 56: andrew_j_w; p. 58: avinashkunnath; p. 63: willwhitedc; p. 65: tiny_packages; p. 68: coolinsights; p. 69: bjaglin; p. 70: Rev Stan; p. 73: amandabhslater; p. 76: bortescristian; p. 79 bottom: jojo-bean; p. 80: bixentro: p. 82: kevinsays; p. 83: Panegyrics of Granovetter; p. 87: damo1977; p. 89:wwarby; p. 91: OpenEnglishWeb; p. 93: Fiona Bradley; p. 94: Gord Bell; p. 96: minor9th; p. 101: DFSHAW; p. 103: gilbrit; p. 104: Djenan; p. 106: _dChris; p. 107: ahisgett; p. 109: WordRidden; p. 110: heatheronhertravels; p. 111: stefo; p. 113: Matt from London; p. 115: jig o'dance; p. 116: Jim Linwood; p. 118: Cleaner Croydon; p. 119: LindaH; p. 127: Mikelo; p. 144: Vic Lic; p. 145: reverendlukewarm; p. 152: terminal5insider; p. 161: Crystian Cruz; p. 164: michaelaion.

TravelNotes

TravelNotes

TravelNotes